The Whole Man

The Whole Man

Studies in Christian Anthropology

by RONALD GREGOR SMITH

THE WESTMINSTER PRESS • PHILADELPHIA

Published in Great Britain under the title *The Free Man*

STANDARD BOOK NO. 664-24851-9

LIBRARY OF CONGRESS CATALOG CARD No. 69-14819

PUBLISHED BY THE WESTMINSTER PRESS®
PHILADELPHIA, PENNSYLVANIA

PRINTED IN THE UNITED STATES OF AMERICA

CONTENTS

ACKNOWLEDGEMENTS

The Author and publishers wish to acknowledge their
indebtedness for permission to use copyright material
contained in this volume as follows:
from *Sermons to Intellectuals* edited by Franklin H. Littell and
published by The Macmillan Company, New York (1963);
from *The Christian Scholar* XLIII, March 1960;
from a symposium entitled *Conflicting Images of Man*
edited by William Nicholls and published by Seabury Press,
New York (1966); from the Australian student journal
Crux Volume IV, 1965; from *New Christian*, March 1966.

Preface

When *The New Man: Christianity and Man's Coming of Age* was published in 1956, I little guessed that it was to be (as the Bishop of Woolwich has recently called it) a 'genuine harbinger' of a great many books in the same field. *The New Man* is long out of print, and when the question of re-printing it arose, it seemed to me that I should expand it somewhat, with the help of various essays and papers which I had prepared for one occasion or another since 1956.

Then, under the expert and friendly scrutiny of Dr Paul Meacham of the Westminster Press, Philadelphia, it became clear that, whatever the historical interest of the whole of *The New Man*, there were other essays which could help to clarify some of the issues. In the end the present volume has come into being, containing slightly revised versions of the last three chapters of *The New Man*, and seven new chapters. These arose out of a variety of occasions, ranging from a talk for the Teacher-Chaplain Group in Greenock, Scotland, to a lecture prepared in February 1967 for the annual *Dozententag* arranged by the theologians of Heidelberg University for their colleagues in all faculties.

The changes I have made do not affect the substance of my argument. For instance, I can now take it for granted that readers interested in the theology of recent decades know something of the main thinkers. Thus I no longer need to introduce the name of Dietrich Bonhoeffer with such elaborate care, or to safeguard the good name of Rudolf Bultmann from the prejudices of ignorance. Again, I am happy to record that my comments on the Roman Catholic Church have had to be considerably modified. It is becoming more and more apparent that the cleavages which do exist no longer run along confessional lines. The point at which the dividing of the spirits takes place can be variously described: in terms of the title of the present book it can be located in the view of man and his freedom.

My theme is the clash between traditional Christian ways of thinking and understanding faith, and modern secular styles. My aim has been to understand the reality of Christian faith in a way which makes sense for our secular world. My general approach might be called 'anthropological', by way, that is to say, of the phenomena of man's own experience: it is a theological anthropology rather than a dogmatic theology which I desire to sketch here. I need hardly add that to talk about man, and especially to see man as a question for himself, does not exclude the reality of the great traditional themes of theology. On the contrary, I hope that the present approach will allow that reality to be disclosed more effectively than the traditional formulations are able to do for the majority of people in our time.

Of the individual chapters, it remains to be said that Chapter I was originally given as a talk to a Student Christian Movement conference at Swanwick, Derbyshire, in 1961, and was published in *Sermons to Intellectuals*, edited by Franklin H. Littell, The Macmillan Company, New York (1963), and appears here by courtesy of The Macmillan Company. Chapter II was originally presented to a conference on 'The Meaning of the Secular' at the Ecumenical Institute, Bossey, Switzerland, in 1958, and appeared as 'A Theological Perspective of the Secular' in *The Christian Scholar*, XLIII, March 1960. Chapter III was written for a symposium entitled *Conflicting Images of Man*, edited by William Nicholls, Seabury Press, New York (1966), and appears here by kind permission of The Seabury Press. Chapters IV, V and VI are respectively Chapters 3, 4 and 5 of *The New Man*, S.C.M. Press, London, and Harper & Row, New York (1956). Chapter

VII is based upon a paper originally given to the Teacher-Chaplain Group associated with the schools in Greenock, and is hitherto unpublished. Chapter VIII was originally prepared for a group of students in the University of Chicago in 1964, and has hitherto appeared in the Australian student journal, *Crux*, IV, 1965. Chapter IX was written for the March, 1966 number of the journal *New Christian*, and thanks are due to the editor for permission to publish it here. Lastly, Chapter X was prepared for the *Dozententag* of the University of Heidelberg in February, 1967, during my time as Visiting Professor there, and is hitherto unpublished.

Thanks are due individually and collectively to all the editors who have allowed me to make new use of the material. In particular, I have great pleasure in recording my gratitude to Mrs W. A. R. Collins, of Messrs Collins, for her tactful encouragement, and to Dr Paul Meacham, Religious Editor of the Westminster Press, for his generous and wise advice and active help in the making of this book.

University of Glasgow　　　　　　　　　　　　　　　　　　R.G.S.
Easter 1968

I

Faith and the Freedom of Man

Of current misconceptions about faith perhaps the commonest is that faith requires some special talent or even a special taste—similar to a liking for caviare or an appreciation of the music of Stravinsky. An acquaintance of mine who is of great repute in his own sphere thought it a matter of course that faith involved a claim to a kind of private line to the Almighty, as he put it.

Others, more sophisticated, think that faith is a kind of irrationalist trick, an illegitimate attempt to find a short-cut through a jungle impassable to honest reason.

But perhaps the commonest complication which you find among the most cultivated of the despisers of religion, or the enquirers concerning its credentials, is that faith is regarded as just one more, perhaps the chief, of the burdens which you are required to carry if you want to be a Christian. They understand that you are required to love everybody; that you are to be amiable and optimistic—in general, more and more of a paragon; and then, on top of all this, you are required to have faith. Faith is the really differentiating burden which is laid on top of all the others. No wonder that it often becomes the last straw that breaks the camel's back!

Against all this I should say that there is an ultimate simplicity in faith. And I think that anyone with some experience of the world beyond the twilit world of the universities, where ideas so easily become spectres and incubi, could agree that there are in fact people everywhere, ordinary people, whose life is quite transparent: they are simply living in faith.

I do not want to forget these people, as I launch out with you now. I much hope that when we have come through—whether 'through' means just this hour, or who knows what days or years of struggle—we shall also reach that kind of simplicity in our faith.

But whether we like it or not, just because we have entered the world of ideas, and their history and interaction, and the world of self-conscious appraisal, we have in fact left that world of simple faith behind us. And all around us, as well as in us, there are other worlds, and in particular the world without faith, the secular world, as we call it, the world which gets along perfectly well without God, which manages its own affairs, better or worse, on its own responsibility, and which, even if it manages them worse and worse, is still unable to find any other help, or any other way than just how it has begun—without reference to God.

Now I think that there is a real connexion between Christian faith and this independence of the world. I think that it is a proper consequence of a properly held Christian faith that there should be this autonomy of the world—its freedom to go its own way, even if this freedom involves, again and again, a departure from the very ground of faith.

But I can explain what I mean by this apparently unreligious reflection only after I have tried to get at the ground of faith. You may have noticed, I have already quietly slipped in the word 'Christian'. I am talking about specifically *Christian* faith. I think that the word 'faith' can be used in other contexts. For instance, we can legitimately say that we believe in so-and-so, or that a physicist believes in the regularity of nature when he makes, or repeats, an experiment. Nor should I wish to deprive adherents of other religions of the use of this word, to believe, to have faith. Nevertheless, not only in our own historical context, but also in the nature of the thing, Christian faith is faith *par excellence*. It is not an accident, nor a sign of mere intolerance, that quite early in the history of Christianity, in the letters of St Paul, even, and quite clearly in the Acts of the Apostles, the word faith is used absolutely of Christian faith. Stephen, for instance, is called 'a man full of faith' (Acts 6.5), and St Paul on his journeys is described as exhorting the new disciples 'to continue in the faith' (Acts 14.22).

If I now ask, what does this summary word mean, precisely, then the provisional answer can only be that faith is co-terminous with all that Christianity is. Then the questions rise quick and fast. Are we talking about something that goes on in you, or something that comes to you from outside yourself? Is this faith something *by* which you believe, or something *in* which (or simply which) you believe? Is it a state of your soul, or, at the other extreme, is it a body of teaching, doctrines, dogmas, confessions, standards, to which you subscribe? Is it an addition to the things you can learn about God, the world, and yourself, by means of your unaided reason? And if it is such an addition, is it a completion or fulfilment of these first things, or does it go against them, so that it might have to be called in some sense an irrational thing? In what sense are we to take those notorious words, *credo quia absurdum*, which have been often alleged to have been said by Tertullian, but which are not to be found in that form in his extant writings? Are we really talking of something which passes comprehension? Or if there is a paradox here, can it be sustained, and not simply written off as a logical contradiction?

There are more refined forms still of these questions: for instance, whether faith may be fully described in psychological terms, and so reduced to an anthropology; or whether faith is inevitably bound up with a specific metaphysic, and that normally means the view inherited from mediaeval scholasticism of a compound structure of being, the realm of nature and the realm of supernature, which you must first accept if you are to find a place for faith.

Now questions of this kind do have their place in a study of faith because of a prior fact about faith. It is this. Faith is essentially historical. By that I mean two things. First, faith arises as a consequence of certain events in history, and second, these historical events constitute the content of faith. To put it in even more concrete and positive terms, faith is (in Bultmann's words) 'the obedient submission to God's revelation in the word of proclamation'. To put it still more strictly, this proclaimed word, which we find at the very heart of the Christian events, is the word through Christ of God's forgiveness of our sins. But this word is not simply a statement, which can then be set down along with other similar propositions, which we have then to subscribe to. But it is a historical word, a word which is lived: rather, it is a historical action, given in a revelatory event, namely, the event of the life and death of Jesus. And faith, which is submission to this event, is likewise an action. It is a free decision on your part, in the totality of your historical being. But just because it is a decision of yours when faced with the question put to you in this lived word, Jesus, by God, this decision is at the same time and in the same action something done to you. The faith is yours, but it is also created in you. It takes its shape in your life in accordance with the content which it already has as the historical Word of God. So to live *in* faith is to live *by* that historical Word which both demands your response and effects upon you God's liberating forgiveness. Faith may therefore now be defined as the free response to the forgiving word of God which frees us to live in the world for God's future.

If you ask, 'How can we call our response a free response, if it is the forgiving word which sets us free?' then I can only reply by pointing to our actual historical situation. We are free to decide, for or against this word. If we decide for it, then our life is henceforth qualified and determined by this free decision. Your life will never be the same again. It is henceforth qualified by the historical Word of God. And this means that a shift has taken place in the totality of your being. You recognize and acknowledge, simultaneously with your own responsibility, your utter dependence upon God. But this does not eliminate your freedom. It sets you on a new way. This new way is not out of your world. But you are as it were taken out of your world by this free submission, and simultaneously put back in again. Nothing less than the totality of your historical existence is at stake. But this historical existence of yours is not destroyed. It is not just veneered over with a gloss of mystical feelings. Nor is some extra quality added to your life, a strange pseudo-something called grace poured into your soul. But you have made a decision, in relation to a constellation of historical events, by which henceforth you are ready to live your life. But this does not mean that you have now been given something which you henceforth possess, either in the form of a new inward experience, a state of soul, or in the form of a series of doctrines. But you are now set in a new relation to yourself and to your world by God.

I nearly said, forgive me, that it is as simple as that. But I am conscious that we have not penetrated to the ultimate simplicity of faith. Perhaps, indeed, with our refined and self-conscious ways people like us, or at least like myself, will never find that faith is a simple thing, till the moment comes when faith is replaced by sight. And then, of course, there is no more need for faith.

Now it is, I think, indisputable that the descriptions which faith gives of itself through history do in fact change. Faith seeks to understand itself, and seeks to express itself, in the changing circumstances of history, and so it is not surprising that it should appear differently at different times. It can even misunderstand itself—and if it does this for long enough then it can lose itself, and turn into something else. But it is also true that unless faith is constantly understanding itself anew in new

15

circumstances it will not be true to itself. For the free decision of faith has to be constantly renewed, in face of its own doubts (which are an integral part of it), in face of its constant, though constantly varying, temptations, and in face of the ever new opportunities which it has of being tested against the questions and demands of its historical circumstances.

I should like to take two examples of this self-understanding of faith, one traditional, and one modern, by which we can throw the basic matter into relief. The first, traditional view is the mediaeval view of faith as consisting of three distinct parts, which follow in chronological sequence: the first element is that of *notitia*, or knowledge. The second is *assensus*, or assent. And the third is *fiducia*, or trust. First you get knowledge, then you give your assent to it, and finally you trust in it. Now it is easy to be impatient with this kind of formal analysis; and I myself am prepared to criticize it quite severely. But the point of the criticism I should make is not that the scholastic thinkers desired to express the reasonableness of faith, which remained reasonable even in the ultimate analysis—in the sense that though faith in the end passed beyond the scope of the natural reason it was never *irrational*. For I think, with them, that Christianity is not simply to be charged with being irrational, or merely arbitrary. My point of criticism of this threefold distinction is rather at the assumption which lies behind it. It is this: the assumption that the faith we are called to accept is capable of being described in a series of propositions, or in a collection of pieces of information, such as you find put down in the creeds of the Church, or in the minutes of ecumenical councils, or, for that matter, of Lambeth Conferences or presbytery meetings or general assemblies. The *notitia* which is the first stage in the acceptance of faith is a series of assertions which have behind them the authority of the Church. This authority is admittedly derived from the authoritative revelation. But—and this is where I find my difficulty—this revelation itself is regarded as a pronouncement, or a series of pronouncements, about the being of God and the life of man. The power of faith is therefore, on this view of revelation, confined to the one deep but strange channel of what is basically a collection of arbitrary messages, which you are authoritatively asked to accept. In effect, the authority is the authority of man. It is the claim which logically ends in the claim to infallibility made by a historical institution. It does not matter at this point whether your obedience is to the Pope or to the Bible. Neither authority can claim the proper obedience of faith. The only claimant is God in his word, and by his word, let me repeat, is meant the liberating word of forgiveness in Christ.

Here, then, we see, in this traditional analysis, an understanding of faith which tries to evade the ground of faith. The ground is the living historical Word.

Now the modern example. Here the difficulty in the traditional view is met by an extreme view which is also, to my mind, unacceptable.

This modern view is very clear that faith is not to be equated with knowledge by inference and argument. You cannot express God. You can only address him. Knowledge by description and inference is replaced by direct knowledge. The whole emphasis is laid upon trust, upon knowing God as you know another person. The I meets the Thou. It is not the God of the philosophers, the God of ideas, the God who is an idea, no more than an idea, but the living God, the God of Abraham, who is the living partner in a living faith. You meet him in a direct encounter. There is a personal presence, in which you speak not of 'knowing about', but simply knowing. Here, therefore, faith is quite simply equated with trust. You trust in the living God, who is entirely self-authenticating in the actual moment of encounter. To quote John Baillie's Gifford Lectures, *The Sense of the Presence of God*, page 18, 'Characteristically and primarily faith is faith in God, confidence in him rather than the uttering of

17

judgements concerning him'.[1] Or to quote an even more extreme statement by the one from whom among modern
thinkers John Baillie has learned most for this way of speaking,
Martin Buber, in *The Eclipse of God*, page 40, 'It is not necessary to
know something about God in order really to believe in him'.[2]

Now far be it from me to wish to throw overboard the insights which have been regained for Christendom, such as are
illustrated in the writings of Martin Buber, with whose thought
I have had so much to do for more than twenty-five years now.
If we classify his thought as personalism, we must never forget
that in an irreducible way the Christian does encounter in his
faith a God who, whatever else he is, is also, or at least, in some
sense personal.

But what I am bound to say is that this kind of personalist
equation of faith with a directness or immediacy of meeting
with God does not do justice to the historicity of faith. Faith—
let me repeat—is obedient submission to God's revelation in the
word of the kerygma or proclamation. If you wish to sum it up
in the one word trust, as I think you can, then you must always
add that it is trust in one who is trustworthy, who has disclosed
himself as trustworthy—and with this addition you are at once
thrown back into the historical situation, back to the events re-
corded in the Bible, and back to the whole ambiguous history of
Christianity—ambiguous both in the *kerygma*, and in its ongoing history right into your own life. You cannot halt at the
immediacy of an encounter and say, 'Here is the ultimate simplicity of faith.' For, once again, faith arises in virtue of certain
historical events, events which themselves shape the faith which
you enter upon. These events cannot be discarded, once they
have been used, as a kind of accidental scaffolding by means of
which you spider your way to the pinnacle of faith.

[1]Oxford University Press 1962.
[2]Victor Gollancz, London 1953 and Harper Torchbooks, New York 1957.

Now I do not think that Martin Buber is either a mystic or a pantheist, or that his account of faith is merely subjective; or that John Baillie's account of faith is lacking in a true evangelical zeal. But I do say that both of them tend to empty faith of its essential historicity. In Martin Buber, especially, you have the paradoxical situation that with all his immense and acute historical sense, both in his work on the biblical documents, and his involvement at every point of his life with intense and even dramatic historical issues, there is at the very heart of his thinking a kind of vacuum: an abstraction from the real historical situation. So much of what he has to say is right and valuable, and needs to be said; yet what he does not say is absolutely cardinal, namely, that in Christ we have the historical offer of a faith which binds us both to our history and to God the Lord of that history.

With these two examples in our mind we can move to some sort of conclusion. It should be clear enough that faith is not something you possess, but a relation into which you enter. It should also be clear that though faith is ineluctably historical, in its origin and in its unfolding, it is not something that you can inherit, from your father or your teachers or by any other claim upon a tradition. The tradition is dormant until you have made your own decision and so entered upon the inheritance.

Two other things must be briefly mentioned. The first is the question of paradox, and the second is the question of secularism.

First, paradox: I can put this vast matter quite briefly for our present purpose. For Christian faith there is only one paradox. It is the forgiving action of God in Christ. This is not irrational or absurd. You know very well what forgiveness is. What Christian faith responds to is the proclaiming of forgiveness by God through Christ in his life and death. This is not a logical contradiction at all. But it is the unheard-of and unimaginable entry of God into human life in his absolute being for men. I cannot go here into the intricate and fascinating work of New Testament scholars who have tried with more or less success to keep this insight free of the encumbrances of traditional modes of thinking and of inevitable error. All I wish to say is that this single paradox is wholly grounded in Christ. He is the ground of our faith. He who was in his life on earth the witness of faith is also through his absolute being for others the ground and basis of faith. Christ is not *simpliciter* God. But he is the Word of God, entered into human being, and freeing us for a life of love, in faith.

I cannot give you any grounds for this faith, external to the one ground, Christ himself. He is the beginning of the way of faith, and he is also the end.

But that end is not yet. We can rightly say that the end is anticipated in faith. In a fundamental sense we have already passed in faith even the last trial of faith, which is death. It is all over, and we live in faith as though nothing mattered. But we cannot be indifferent. For faith casts us back into the world.

And this brings me to my last point, secularism. I said at the beginning that there is a real connexion between Christian faith and the independence of the world. The independence of the world is a contemporary fact. We could all give innumerable examples of how men live their lives today without reference to God. And indeed this is not a new phenomenon. We are living at the end of an age which began with immense hopes, with a sense of immense liberation from outmoded forms of belief. What is the significance of this? It is not possible to say either that it is a mere rebellion against God, or that it is a simple necessity of historical development. For history remains ambiguous, and a mystery till the end. None of us can see the whole meaning of it. But what we can say derives from the nature of Christian faith. The description of faith which I have given you involves man's freedom to decide. And with his decision for faith, as it has been made in the past, one of the accompaniments was the liberation of the world. Man recognised and acknowledged his responsibility for history. The world was no longer seen as a mythological theatre for the battle between good and evil spirits. The world of gnosis as well as the world of mythological objectifying were exorcised. The world became man's, in faith. It was not merely de-mythologized by Christ, it was de-divinized. In this way man was able to become the decider of his own future. He was liberated from magic spells and from incomprehensible authority.

All this was implicit in the free acceptance of the Word from God, which freed man from anxiety about himself and the world. God's action in Christ has therefore to be seen as a separation as well as an advent. The fact that his Word comes contains the faith that he is also not of this world. Men are now invited to be heirs, to grow up, and to accept their responsibility for the world. For Christian faith takes you right into history, and it makes you responsible for history, as the place where God is. But God is not in the historical world as a part of the world; nor on the other hand is he merely cut off from the world. It is here, in the heart of Christian faith, that the ambiguity of history is found at its most potent. For faith affirms the presence of God in history which at its climax is simultaneously an absence of God. This is the special dialectic of faith, which it encounters in the historical situation, that is, in the Word made flesh, the conjoined presence and absence of God. This is the nearest to directness which you get in Christianity, and its qualifying term is always faith: we believe in God through Christ. This is what Dietrich Bonhoeffer means in that strange sentence in one of his last letters from prison, where he says, 'God teaches us to live in the world without God'. This intense dialectic is sustained at the very centre of Christianity as its proper scandal and stumbling-block; and the only way of sustaining it is faith.

In view of all this it is not surprising that you should find today, in spite of every anxiety, a tremendous exhilaration in the powers of man. For these powers are no longer infected by the ancient fear of devils or angels. They are rightly regarded as powers which are part of man's self-responsibility. Christian faith recognizes them as powers of freedom, which are intrinsic to the givenness of all men's gifts. The Christian believer is captivated by the mystery of the existence of the world and his own existence. (He is an ontologist at heart; he cannot think the idea of God without believing the Presence.) It is the Christian's duty—or rather, he cannot avoid believing, that in this free responsibility which he has, the element of givenness runs through everything: through his hopes and enterprises, through his fears and doubts, and through his inklings of the glory. This givenness is the ground of his hope: the givenness of history, and especially of the historical phenomenon of Jesus as the Word. This hope can of course be expressed in many different ways, and like faith it has taken a great variety of forms in the course of history. And in our own time, in which secularism is the form into which everything turns—in the words of the Dutch philosopher van Peursen, 'there are no more transcendental things, but just worldly things'—the question certainly faces us, whether we are not left with a completely intramundane and functional world. Has the secularist movement not led us to mere relativism and immanentism in all our judgements? Where is the hope, then?

I can only repeat, hope takes many forms. And the form which it might take today is one in which the autonomy of this world is seen as sustained by the tension which may issue in a new theonomy—God not *in* the world, nor *over* the world as a metaphysical substance, but God through Christ in the world, present to faith.

I have said the Christian faith is not irrational. At the same time, there is no limit set. The Christian believes through Christ that everything is reconciled to God. For we believe that

Christ is the perfecter as well as the pioneer of our faith. So we believe that a time like the present, which is especially full of anxiety about the future of history, is especially a time in which faith may come into its own. Faith too has a future: God's future; and in this ultimate recourse there is a kind of certainty: the only certainty available to faith, the certainty of a personal and fighting faith.

II

Man in his Wholeness

In attempting to present what I call 'a theological perspective of the secular', I am well aware that I may obtain for my reward the worst of two worlds. I have to run the gauntlet between certain opposing theories and positions of theologians on the one side, and of self-contained, or at least untheological, secularists on the other side. I am ready to take this risk, and to do it in a sense without weapons, in a defenceless manner, even if I seem rather naïve and unsystematic to the theologians, and rather arbitrary, positivist, and naïve as well, to the secularists.

In a sense I do not choose this approach, but it is chosen for me by the fact that I consider myself to be simultaneously some kind of theologian, and immersed willy-nilly in secular styles of apprehension and living.

It follows from this that I have no intention of attempting any kind of systematic assemblage of theological views as a kind of weapon with which to belabour the secularist into unconsciousness and possible submission. Even if I thought this kind of systematization were central to the work of theology, which I do not, I still should not undertake it here, for in doing so I should be untrue to the other side of the reality which we all face, namely the secular style in which we all share.

My fundamental assumption is that the world which the theologian looks at and the world which the secularist looks at are one and the same. I do not argue this; I accept it as the situation in which I personally find myself. Certainly this one world can be read differently, and this is what constitutes our particular problem. But if we were to leave it there and recognize the differences as determinative and the oneness of the world and therefore the oneness of the truth as merely incidental and even a matter of indifference, then I think we might as well give up hope altogether. And to give up hope means to push man out of the centre of the picture and merely to use him for some other purpose extraneous to his actual being.

The centre of the picture is man. I mean this in a quite particular sense, I hope a sense which the theologians proper will not simply decry as mere anthropology and which the secularists so-called will not want to write off as veiled reactionism. Père Teilhard, that remarkable Jesuit scientist and scholar, one of the rare examples in our time of the liberally-minded *Wissenschaftler*, writes of modern man in his posthumous work, *The Phenomenon of Man*: 'We have become aware that in the great game that is being played we are the players as well as the cards and the stakes.'[1] Two hundred years ago in the heyday of the Enlightenment, Johann Georg Hamann, the friend and critic of Kant, said that the way of man leads through the descent to hell of self-knowledge, *die Höllenfahrt der Selbsterkenntnis*. Both these men held in their relatively different ways to a Christian confession of faith. Yet both of them have what is to my mind the characteristic modern insight, namely that it is man, individual man, but also man in his wholeness as man, who is the real theme of man's interest. For these two, Teilhard and Hamann alike, it is man's self-awareness that constitutes man as man, and it is this self-conscious man who both makes and constitutes the reality of history.

My subject is therefore this man: man in his wholeness as man, and man as responsible for history. This for me is the cen-

---

[1]Pierre Teilhard de Chardin *The Phenomenon of Man* trs. by Bernard Wall, Collins, London, and Harper & Brothers, New York 1959. Also available in Fontana.

tral and inclusive reality which takes in the material alike of theology and of secularism.

I must now attempt a definition of what I mean by theology. It is easier to say what it is not. Theology is not simply the elaboration of propositions or doctrines about God. Nor is it the assertion or the maintenance of a specific world-view or a metaphysic against some other. A battle of ideologies may take place in the domestic circles of theology, but it is better conducted behind closed doors. In the last resort this is not the central task of theology. It is regrettable that the Church in many places should be so ready to identify itself with some kind of ideology that it sees its task to consist in overthrowing some other ideology. It is possible that Marxism may be an enemy to be laid low, more especially as Marxism is historically so near a relation of Christian points of view; but it is indisputable that the Marxist himself, if he is to be considered as an enemy, can only be faced as such in the ultimate Christian situation, which is not one of ideologies but of faith, hope, and love. Of course the battle of concepts has gone on in one form or another throughout the life of Christianity. I think for instance of the partner concepts of the holy and the profane, or of the more refined partners of the natural and the supernatural, or of the concepts already so confusedly intermingled in the thought-world of the New Testament, the concepts of other-worldly and this-worldly. But the struggles for clarification which have gone on in these various battles have always been secondary to the main issue.

This main issue I put provisionally in the form of a question: is the controlling power in human life made by men, or not? My own answer, as any real answer, rests upon a decision. My decision is that the primary and ultimately controlling power is not made by men but is given to men.

Is this the dividing line? Are all theologians determined by response to a givenness whereas all secularists are determined by a particular understanding of free and creative humanness?

26

If we were simply fighting a battle with a clearly defined enemy, then this kind of dividing line might be accepted. Unfortunately I find myself here to be my own enemy as well, and no such neat division is possible. For the secularist can well say that he too of course works from a givenness, only he does not immediately claim for this givenness any kind of heteronomous or spiritualist or sacral sanction such as he might charge the theologian with possessing, or thinking he possesses, in the form of an unprovable revelation; while the theologian on the other hand might equally say that he too assigns a very important place, indeed in a specific sense the ultimate place, to free and creative humanness. I think that with varied reservations most theologians would for instance be ready to endorse the dictum of Max Scheler, who spoke of the characteristic achievement of Europe as consisting in the *Wertsetzung der freien Persönlichkeit*, which we might translate as 'the establishing of free personality as *the* value.'

It is perhaps hardly necessary to point out—certainly not to the theologians and probably not to the secularists either, though in each case the assessment of the situation is a different one—that in the present state of theology it is extremely difficult to get solid grounds of agreement. The fact is that ever since the *Aufklärung* and strictly speaking even further back, ever since the break of Europe with its own so-called mediaeval period, theology has been in a state of immense, and one must also add, sometimes chaotic, motion. Sometimes this has meant that theology has, from its aspect as a human science, either inaugurated or reflected changes in the understanding of man and the world. The rise of strict literary criticism for instance is very much bound up with the story of biblical exegesis. The chief problem of our time, the nature of history, has likewise been brought into the forefront and even, as I shall mention later in the biblical context, been brought into being by christological necessities. On the other hand this chaotic motion has sometimes looked—especially, I might add, to a rather unhistorical assessment—like the mere death-throes of theology. For instance the retreat of theology before certain developing views of the world, especially in the nineteenth century the beginnings of evolutionary views, certainly looked to the theologians of that time and to their secularist opponents like the abandonment of vital positions. The matter was not helped by the bad temper, indeed the virulence, with which the battle was waged and the grudging manner in which the Church accepted defeat. And if we look at the present time, quite apart from what I might call standard differences of Confessional attitudes, there are differences in standpoint between leading Protestant theologians, for instance between Karl Barth and Rudolf Bultmann, which might well seem to an outsider to spell the bankruptcy of theology: when you are faced with what seems in Barth to be the last magnificent fling of a heteronomous dogmatism and in Bultmann to be the last reduction of theology to a ghostly anthropology, emptied of all historical strength.

But let me return to the question I have asked: is the controlling power in human life made by men or given to them? The theologian answers, it is given; and he adds, it is given to men in such a way that it is also made by them. That is, man is both recipient and maker, both controlled, limited, and the controller, in freedom, in a freedom which has the real substance of freedom, and that means, is unlimited. It is in this paradoxical situation where man recognizes both his dependence and his independence, his being controlled and his controlling, his being both limited and unlimited, that the main theological issue lies, so far as the perspective leads towards the meaning of the secular.

I put it another way. The basic question for theology is neither What are we to do? nor How are we to think of things? but Whence do we receive? That is to say, it is neither a simple manual or code of conduct nor indeed any kind of action which is the first concern of theology. (This of course includes, in our particular perspective, the whole concern of Christianity, for theology formally speaking is just the working out of what Christians believe). Nor again is the prime concern of theology any structure of thought. It is easy for theologians to go off the rails here and to get involved in endless and delightful discussions about the relation of faith and reason. All I should like to say about this matter is that while dogmatics is an absolutely essential discipline for Christianity, especially as the internal or domestic effort to understand what it is concerned with, though also as the effort to make clear to the non-Christian what its general intention and scope are, so that it may make clear what is the minimum space it requires as a breathing-space in the world—a true dogmatics must never be equated with a structure or system of thought consisting of a series of propositions, whether interlinked or not, about God and the world. But a true theological concern, and therefore the guiding concern for a true dogmatics, has to do neither with action in itself nor with thought in itself but with this question, Whence do we receive? The theological key word here is grace. In less strict but more contemporary language—at least in the language of writers like Martin Buber and Karl Jaspers—the key word would be otherness. By these words, grace and otherness, I wish to indicate the theological concern which is nothing else but a kind of witnessing or pointing: the ultimate theological concern is with men as having to do with what is not themselves, with what they do not and never can possess at all, as part of their self-equipment or as material for their self-mastery, but with what comes to them all the time from beyond themselves.

If I may put the matter at its lowest estimate, we may say that theology begins with the recognition of God as being not-man, as being over against man. Simultaneously Christian theology recognizes this otherness as pressing in upon man, and again to put it at its lowest, as a kind of disturbance. It would be fairly simple at this point to elevate this preliminary suggestion in terms of one or the other traditional or fashionable theological or philosophical or religious *Begrifflichkeiten* or conceptual structures. For instance Rudolf Otto, having learned much from Schleiermacher, speaks here of the numinous: a rationalist like St Thomas Aquinas speaks of the life of nature being completed by grace; Karl Barth or his real master, Kierkegaard, speaks of the infinite qualitative difference between God and man. I certainly would not wish to decry the achievement of any one of those great doctors of theology. But I must try to keep to the fundamental naïvety which seems to me to be essential if there is to be real conversation between our different positions. And so I say that this recognition of a given otherness, which is at the same time a disturbance, a question, addressed to man's being, is from the Christian point of view by no means something that takes place in isolation or abstraction. It takes place in this world which is also in a special sense man's world. The God that Christian theology speaks about here is not God in isolation but God in the world. Theology here faces intellectually its one and only problem. Christian faith on the other hand does not face any problems but simply decides to go a certain way. To Christian faith it is God in the world and for the world who constitutes the ground of action and understanding. But Christian theology has to try to speak about this givenness in such a way that, while God is given in and for the world, at the same time he is recognized as distinct from the world, and therefore, while given in the phenomena of the world, i.e., in its structures and events and even in human persons in their relationships, yet he is never recognized as a phenomenon of the world. In Barth's language, God is always subject; that is, he can never be an object of experience if by experience you mean the direct perceptual apprehension of an object among other objects in the world.

This means that simultaneously with the recognition of

God's presence the theologian recognizes that no immediacy is possible. God cannot be inferred in the world. He cannot be demonstrated. His existence cannot be proved. Nor on the other hand can we take refuge in the identification of his presence with a pantheist position. God's presence is apprehended rather as an action or event in and through the structures of the world. Strictly speaking God cannot be seen, nor can he be brought in as the conclusion of an argument. While it is in the human situation that his presence is recognized, yet it is not in nature or history as rounded and completed entities in and for themselves that this recognition takes place. The traditional and to some extent positive statement which emerges at the end of these negatives is that God's presence in the human situation is apprehended in faith.

I am not able to say much here in a direct way about the meaning of faith. A remarkable analysis of the meaning of faith has been given by Gerhard Ebeling in his *Das Wesen des christlichen Glaubens*. I quote some sentences from this work which can be taken as a kind of summary of what I have said so far:

> Man's true freedom consists in his receiving himself from elsewhere, that he does not owe it to himself that he is, that he is not his own creator and thus cannot free himself from himself. . . . For it is the mystery of human personal being that it is summoned from elsewhere, that it exists in response and as response, and that therefore man is wholly himself when he is not caught up in himself, but has the real ground of his life outside himself.[1]

This much I may add, that faith is basically a decision about your life which involves you in a recognition of this otherness

[1]Gerhard Ebeling *Das Wesen des christlichen Glaubens* J. C. B. Mohr, Tübingen 1959, p145: English translation *The Nature of Faith* Collins, London and Fortress Press, Philadelphia 1961, p115. Also available in Collins Fontana Library.

which presses in upon you. The focus of this otherness is the historical figure of Jesus, otherwise pregnantly described as the Word which God has uttered, and that means the Word which God has done in historical human circumstances. I am not ignoring this historical focus if I say that the work of theology is to understand what faith means. For faith is simply the reaction of man to God's action. It is the response of man to the question which rises up in man's own being, the question of the source and goal of man's particular being.

Implicit in what I have said are one or two matters, secondary decisions you might call them, which I mention in passing. First, in what I have said I have cut myself adrift from a great deal of traditional theologizing, in particular what I would call the theology of demonstration or the whole system of natural theology. I do not deny a place to a certain kind of 'natural' theology, an extra-Christian understanding of or even an approach to God. But as a Christian I am not prepared to speak about God except in terms of a decision of faith about his presence in the world. I am also not able to speak about God in any kind of spiritualizing terms, whether in old-fashioned allegorizing or more fashionable typologizing or in terms of a metaphysical system. It is God in the world, in this one world, whose presence to faith I should put as the kind of basic minimum of Christian apprehension.

This brings me, I think and hope, near to the expression of the secularist style of thinking and living. Let me try to define how it seems to me that the secularist thinker sees the world. I think it is somewhat misleading to speak of the secularist point of view as being basically just a new religion. So far as wholeness in the point of view and zeal for its propagation are concerned, then perhaps there are illustrations of secular enterprise which might carry that title. But it is better to reserve the word religion for phenomena which have a minimum of certain common items, and that minimum I should say includes, besides a

set of convictions, a code of behaviour and some kind of insti-
tutional or organizational set-up. Christianity as a faith is always in conflict with Christianity as a religion, and there is an
important—I should be inclined to say the most important—
sense in which Christian faith includes within itself the permanent protest against its own religious forms and expressions. In
this important sense Christianity understands itself as being
more than a religion, as including within itself the negation of
religion, though permanently destined to carry religion along
with itself, that is, to give form and expression to its own faith
in some kind of concord with traditional and social expectations.

But secularism cannot really be described either as a religion
or as a faith. I think that as a historical description Jaspers's
words are apt when he speaks of the modern 'transformation
of the transcendental conception into a seeing of the world as
immanent movement'; and similarly Gabriel Marcel, when he
speaks in his diary, *Being and Having*, of the radical formula of
autonomy as being summed up in the words, 'I want to run my
own life.'

Both definitions point to a world which is self-contained and
in which man is self-sufficient: there is one world, and man is
the meaning of it. These definitions go further than a simple
description of the historical emergence of secularism, which as
Dr Charles West has said, has meant 'the withdrawal of areas of
thought and life from religious—and finally also from metaphysical—control, and the attempt to understand and live in
these areas in the terms which they alone can offer.'[1] This description is I think true to the historical development, though I
think we may add to it the rather critical remark of Marcel: 'I
am tempted to think that the idea of autonomy is bound up

[1] Dr Charles West, memorandum at a Conference on 'The Meaning of
the Secular' at the Ecumenical Institute, Bossey, Switzerland, September
1959.

with a kind of narrowing or particularization of the subject.'[1]
We might say that the very successes of a secularist standpoint
depend upon a specialization which might well in the long run
destroy even the successes. It is certainly true though—and even
keeping the dangers in mind—that historically speaking a
secularist standpoint allows in principle every area of life to work
out its own purpose according to the procedures and hypo-
theses which are inherent in that area. And again it is true that
this development has meant the freeing of all kinds of human
activities and enterprises from the bond of heteronomous
standpoints. This is the kind of thing which Dietrich Bonhoeffer
recognized, though without properly evaluating: the spontaneous break-away of individual disciplines in ever-increasing
power of self-determination.

All this is to my mind incontrovertible, and I can only explain
the enthusiasm with which Bonhoeffer's remarks have been
taken up (by students of theology more readily than by their
teachers) as reflecting the sense of liberation in many theologians' minds when they find that a noble person and a com-
petent thinker like Bonhoeffer does not feel bound to try to
maintain any of the earlier traditional positions of theology,
e.g. last ditch defence in the wrong ditch or heteronomous
positivism or sheer biblicism and so on. Unfortunately Bonhoeffer did no more than indicate the problem for theology and
secularism in our time. Perhaps the actual course of his life
which involved him, as a believing Christian, in the thick of the
events culminating in the attempt on Hitler's life on July 20,
1944, was the only real answer to a problem which involved not
only intellectual adjustments but also a venture of faith.

But more important, I think, because more pervasive is what
Charles West has called the secularist *style*. This is very difficult to

---

[1]Gabriel Marcel *Being and Having* trs. by Katherine Farrer, Dacre Press, Westminster 1949 and Beacon Press, Boston 1951, p131.

analyze, partly because we are all enveloped in it and partly because it is scarcely ever questioned. But let me try to look at it all the same. It includes a kind of diffident self-awareness, combined with a powerful relativism. It has spread over the whole world, as Ebeling has said, 'like a spring tide,' propagating itself much more quickly and effectively than any of the deliberate traditional Christian missions and even transforming old cultures, such as the Buddhist and Confucian, and thus involving the whole of mankind in a universal uniformity which curiously enough still leaves room for the play of the most ancient and deep-seated animosities and struggles for power.

Here I should like to ask a question of the secularist which is at the same time a question of myself. If this relativism of all experience is so unquestioned and at the same time man is recognized to be his own legislator, working out his purposes as he frames his provisional laws—a reasonable being 'legislating universally for himself' (Marcel)—how can you avoid subsuming man himself under the category of a kind of spontaneous self-decision whose real power comes not from autonomous man but from a kind of immanent teleology of life itself? If you first recognize man's autonomy to be ultimate and determinative and then admit the relativity of everything, do you not drive man himself into a hopeless corner? How can man's autonomy be reconciled with ultimate relativism? Do you not have to give up one or the other, either the autonomy or the relativism? What seems to me to happen in practice is that man as man, man in his wholeness, and man in his sole and absolute responsibility for history, takes second place to a view of the world. Man's own view of the world pushes man himself out of the centre. A kind of intellectual and spiritual suicide takes place. The secularist standpoint seems to contain this contradiction in itself; and with an insufficient grasp of its own assumption about man's autonomy it again and again relapses into various kinds of sub-human or anti-human mythologies. So

35

Marxism and scientism and various technological collectivisms replace the reality of man's life as man. I need hardly say that the critical danger which pervades every social structure today is not over-population nor scientific arrogance, not even the atom bomb, but the fearful assumption that man is there to be managed; and the classic description of that managing and manipulation is to be found in George Orwell's *Nineteen Eighty-four*.

I feel that at this point my hope is betrayed by the very power of secularism which has without any doubt brought so much benefit to society. I can very easily abandon hope. It is possible to adopt the open-eyed despair of a man like Lord Russell, or to assert nothingness and take a kind of cold comfort from the mere assertion. But in the last resort no man can live by despair, but only through despair in hope.

So my question here is, Is secularism because it is tied to a view of the world (relativist, immanent, perfectionist yet pessimistic) not inherently self-destructive? Has it not an inadequate view of man's being, so that in all that it so powerfully plans for man it actually leaves out the dimension of man's paradoxical dependence in freedom, his limited and conditioned being, as the presupposition for his unlimited aspirations? This question does not intend simply to smuggle in the traditional formulas again, such as the need for the supernatural or otherworldly, in order to complete the picture of man by as it were restoring the top story to his house of the universe. But I am suggesting that the inadequacy of the secularist standpoint, as commonly presented, lies not in its concentrating on man and his history in the world but in its not concentrating enough on this fundamental situation. Secularism is not secularist enough. And so it subordinates man to a view of the world in which man's essential freedom is lost.

As I see the situation, the dilemma today is not to be solved by any kind of pathetic return. The age of ecclesiastical heteronomy is, I hope, over for ever. If there are any theologians left who really wish for a return, then we can only hope that they will not forget their church history, and the history is not confined to any church or sect. I should add that this kind of history is not peculiar to the Christian Church, but the temptation to heteronomous action is general to mankind: man is perennially tempted to discern an absolute at work and then to take the easy short-cut of identifying his recognition with that absolute in such a way that he thinks he actually possesses it. To think that you possess the truth or to believe that a doctrine or a system or some other authority can be infallible is the root temptation of man. And it is the temptation which suggests that man—other men—can and must be managed and manipulated.

I have suggested a criticism of the secularist standpoint from within, as it were on its own terms. It would be easy to develop this criticism along lines which are I think familiar to us all. The analyses which have been given to us by such different writers as Martin Buber, Ortega y Gasset, and Hans Urs von Balthasar do not differ essentially: perhaps Buber's elaboration of the two-fold world of man, in the realm of the I-It and the realm of the I-Thou, is the best known and most useful analysis. The loss of the personal realm and with it the loss of true community is the point which is most relevant to our immediate problems. But I do not care to elaborate this. I have often tried it, and it has seemed to me that unless there is already a passionate concern present, whether dormant or outspoken, for the reality of what is meant here, you cannot really hope for a response.

If I may take an example from my own experience, I had the opportunity in the autumn of 1958 of some talks with one or two of the leading officials in the German Democratic Republic, and in my position I was able to be fairly outspoken—without, I hope, overstepping the bounds of common courtesy. Perhaps these bounds are really a constituent part of the realm in whose strength and on whose behalf I was trying to speak, and perhaps

I could only have made myself understood by denying the power in whose name I tried to speak. At any rate, while I found attention, even attentiveness, and a kind of tolerant applause for what I was urging (in this case it happened to be the furthering of exchange of students between Jena and Glasgow), there was a basic and radical and deep cleft between us: there was in effect no personal dialogue, no openness, no trust, no expectation that possibly we might really understand one another. In fairness I must add that when I put forward similar proposals back home in my Faculty meetings in Glasgow, I met with fundamentally the same polite unconcern. In other words I am not talking of Communist peculiarities but of sub-human interests everywhere proliferating, the world of It swamping the world of Thou. And the only hope that I perceive here is in what Buber calls *turning*. I am sorry to say that at this point I can offer no cure for the situation in terms of the situation but only in terms of strange and unpredictable happenings, like the breath of the Spirit or the gift of grace or the vision of some newness actually changing people. Perhaps the recognition of his fundamental loneliness will somehow drive modern man out of himself, and also out of the societies in which only the same fundamental loneliness is to be seen reflected in all their members, and into the situation of real self-assertion and self-decision which I should also describe as the situation of real faith.

One other chief matter remains to be discussed, and that is the connexion between Christianity and secularism. The genesis of the secularist view is to be found in a theological understanding of man and the world. I do not mean this in a merely general sense, for instance that the ideals of the Welfare State arise out of certain Christian ideas such as brotherly love and service of the community, though this is at least partly true. But this kind of generalization is as often a pious substitute for real Christian action. How often can you hear the claim made in popular Christian apologetics that it was Christianity which was responsible for the abolition of the slave trade inside the British Empire; whereas the truth of the matter is so complicated that the only possible generalization seems to me to be that, when a particular historical action is accomplished, the time for it was ripe and it happened. This does not mean that I reduce history to the level of nature, as that in autumn the plums fall from the tree, but it does mean that historical action is an almost unravellable web of many different strands.

The theological understanding of man and the world goes further back and deeper into the forces which play about and in the life of man. Quite briefly, it arises from the nature of faith as you find it expressed in the New Testament. In St Paul's *Epistle to the Galatians* you can find the simplest adumbration of this understanding. I think especially of chapter 4, verses 1-7. Here we find faith described as involving maturity and responsibility for history. The passage is followed by an exhortation to stand fast in the freedom with which Christ has made us free. This freedom of the Christian has a twofold implication. First, the world is released from bondage to the beggarly elements, that is, it is no longer seen as the place of supernatural powers, mythologically conceived. The world, to coin a horrid word, is de-divinized. At the same time the world is seen positively as the place, distinct from God, in which man exerts his free responsibility for it. Luther said, 'The sphere of faith's works is worldly society and its order.' Dilthey has justly said of this remark, 'With this sentence there enters into history one of the greatest organizing thoughts that a man has ever had.' In fact you can say that with Luther's understanding of faith the world is both set free to be itself and also clearly established as the place where man's maturing responsibility has free play. The world becomes for the first time truly historical, that is, the place of man's responsible care. Man is the heir who has come of age and whose care it is to make history. It is in this sense that I have spoken of a givenness which is given in such a way that it is also made by men. Man is set free, but his freedom is guarded by his receptivity. He is free, but he is not God. God is no longer entangled in the world; he removes himself. God was not expelled from the world. Only a certain way of speaking about God and on his behalf has been expelled. And this is a good thing, especially if it reduces an unnecessary tension which arises when Christians act as though they had a vested interest in God and were under the obligation to keep on proving his existence, in a kind of anxiety lest if they ceased he would entirely vanish away. But God has removed himself. The ultimate Christian word for this removing is God's absence as acknowledged in the cry of dereliction from Christ on the cross: 'My God, my God, why hast thou forsaken me?' So the world becomes sheer world. But for the Christian this distinction of God from the world, and so the possibility of history and the whole secular movement in embryo, does not lead to mere or sheer undialectical atheism. Any assertion of the absence of God and even further of his nonexistence among the phenomena of the world is dialectically confronted by the equal assertion of his presence. I am sorry if this sounds like a mere verbal trick, but it cannot be helped. It is really only the believer who can make the atheist assertion. Unfaith and faith go together, and the assurance of faith is only to be found in the possibility of doubt.

I shall not develop this inner dialectic of faith here. For the last question which arises here is more important for our present theme. Let us suppose that this historical source of secularist thought is in fact properly understood as deriving from Christian conceptions and Christian experience. Is it not possible to say, the source does not control the present and future course of man's life? Now if I were merely asking for a dash of piety to be introduced into free historical actions and situations, like the prayer at the opening of the House of Commons or like the Welsh Rugby team singing the hymn 'Abide with me' before they play a match against England, then of course I should not make any claim here. Far less do I make any claim for a dogmatic heteronomy or theocracy. Nevertheless the Christian understanding of man in history, it seems to me, cannot be discarded like a scaffolding. It is in the particular understanding of what man is, in which is included his secular and autonomous responsibility, that I find it impossible merely to see man as developing from one stage to another, discarding as he goes the various earlier insights into his being which had brought him so far on the way. Man is in so far as he receives. He is only so far as he is whole. And this wholeness is only found in relation with others. Man's being is being in relation. This simply cannot be arranged or planned. It happens, it is an event in which man's being is disclosed in the presence of the other. And this disclosure is only possible on the basis of freedom from all ideologies, all views of the world which enclose man without reserve.

An ultimate secularism must be reached. I do not consider that this has happened merely when everything has been separated off into sheer autonomous regions or when everything is subsumed under any ideology or mould of thought whatsoever. But this ultimate secularism is reached only when the secularist process or movement goes to the very end of the road. Freed of all ideologies, in complete freedom man is then left entirely by himself. Then at this end a question still arises in man. The question may bring him to the apprehension of a new theonomy. Professor Kornelis Miskotte, the Dutch theologian, has called the theonomous view the counter-pole to autonomy. I should prefer to speak of it as the waiting answer to the ultimate question which arises at the end of the secularist road. (This end of course may come anywhere any time to the individual.) The question is, Who am I? And the answer comes—in the form of another question—Adam, where art thou? This question, which is the only answer received to man's own last question about himself, is not merely a call of the conscience, the self addressing the self, but it is the liberating word spoken by God in the free historical situation of man. And it liberates man for still deeper autonomy and still richer theonomy. It is only in this way that we can speak of man's eternal being, in that he may be made new again and again in this dialogue. So he is open to the world and history.

This openness to the world, which is the basic prerequisite of free and responsible historical action, is only possible if the world itself is not closed. The freedom of man, which is unlimited, is only possible on the basis of a givenness to which man is bound. Man does not make himself. He is made. Put into more traditional Christian terminology, this means that faith makes the world again what it truly is, the creation of God. It is only because man in faith is freed from the world that he is free for the world. It is the one undivided world which the Christian shares with his fellow-men. It is a historical world, not a world of spectral beings or of over-arching plans. For the Christian the historicity of the world means that the world is entirely open to the future, yet man is without foresight. Strictly speaking, the question about the meaning of history, which can be answered only at the end of history, is an enigma which the Christian faces in faith. Historical living means living in the present in the strength of the future. This means living by hope. And in case there are some theological murmurings at my lack of explicitness about specific Christian assertions, I can willingly add that this faith, which so allows man's freedom and responsibility to be paramount for his history, springs not from the simple disappearance of God from the world but from his veiled appearance in Christ, that is, from his appearance which is simultaneously a veiling, containing also the promise, even the anticipation, of finality.

Again I should like to attempt a summary by quoting from Gerhard Ebeling:

> Because faith does not live on the world, it makes it possible for us to live for the world. Because it puts an end to the

misuse of the world, it opens the way to the right use of the world. Because faith breaks the domination of the world, it gives domination over it and responsibility for it. And because it drives out the liking and the misliking of the world, it creates room for pure joy in the world.[1]

It is in this kind of analysis, and in the power of faith thus understood, that man really comes to himself. In any other analysis he remains a cipher, and if man as man is not absolutely safeguarded, then anything that man undertakes is bound to end in his own destruction. He can only be properly safeguarded, it seems to me, in his inexhaustible freedom and richness of possibility if he is also recognized in his contradictions, his impossible longings as well as his sober achievements, his misery as well as his grandeur, but not one without the other. This is only possible when he recognizes himself as set between God and the world, which is at the same time the setting of God in and for the world. God in man is for the world: this is the essence of Christian belief, it is *Christian* because it is a faith in and through Christ concerning God for the world.

If that faith absolutely disappears, then man is without hope and will cease striking his tents and going out. For you can only go out and go on if you do so in faith.

[1] *op. cit.* p211: English translation p161.

III

Post-Renaissance Man

'Who am I?' asked Dietrich Bonhoeffer in one of his most moving poems, written in a Nazi prison.[1] And like many of the Psalms, which take in the whole world in their course, he too ends with words of commitment:

Whoever I am, thou knowest, O God, I am thine.

Between the question and the answer lies man in his world. Bonhoeffer's view of the world has become the subject of many studies. It contains immensely fruitful insights and ambiguities, but is on the whole too fragmentary and casual to be presented in a systematic form. I make use of his views, here and elsewhere, with deep gratitude, but without feeling under any compulsion to regard him as my mentor.

Certainly it is the ambiguities which are also the most immediately striking thing about the modern view of man and his world. Indeed it cannot really be said that there is a uniform view. The only statement about modern man that might be generally acceptable is that man is more problematic to himself today than at any other time. From the various autonomous disciplines of our time there come forth tentative anthropologies which bear little resemblance to one another, and which take little or no account of what is being said in the neighbour disciplines.

My purpose here is to attempt to present a theological an-

---

[1]Cf. *Letters and Papers from Prison* S.C.M. Press, London, 3rd revised and enlarged edition 1967, pp197*f*. As *Prisoner for God* Macmillan Co., New York 1959.

thropology, with particular reference to what has happened since the Renaissance. By 'theological', however, I do not imply that I wish to impose upon the picture of modern man the propositions of a heteronomous theology. I offer no specific metaphysic, and claim no special authority from any unexamined 'revealed' truths. But I wish to look at the phenomena. I therefore start from the very ambiguities of the empirical, historical situation.

How may we fitly describe the present situation? Man is his own master, and is confident that there are no bounds to his powers. He thinks that he can do anything that he wishes to do. But at the same time he is very short on hope. He plans to reach the moon, but he is afraid that he will not have the time to do so. In the searing words of Kornelis Miskotte, one form of modern nihilism says:

> There is no reality behind any faith or ideal. There is nothing but an abyss of absurd existence. But hail to the summer, the sun, laughter; blessed be life and strength and women! We roam the world with hungry eyes to see everything we can; we want to fly to the moon; there is not time enough to enjoy to the full this terrible life.[1]

Or we may say that man is free, and come of age, but at the same time the slave of the very ideologies which in his freedom he has constructed. And even if he struggles against the absurdity of existence, and recognizes in its very absurdity the call to be himself, as a 'single person' (in Kierkegaard's words), he finds himself in this very recognition continually threatened with immersion in the life of the collective. And this collective is not a mere sociological abstraction, but is the life of habitual conformism, and cultural fundamentalism, and fear, which is common to the entire broken world of what was once Chris-

[1] Kornelis Miskotte *When the Gods are Silent* Collins, London and Harper and Row, New York 1967, p21.

tendom. The threat of this collectivism is also something which modern man desires, as a man who drives round a blind corner on the wrong side desires the threat which lies in ambush for him. He desires it, in order that he may evade the hard demand to be a single person.

There is a fearful ambivalence here, and the man of today does not know where to turn. No analysis, from whatever perspective, is satisfactory which ignores this; and even if the attempt is made to trace a dominant *motif* and possibility for man, no static harmonizing of the contraries can be expected; the ambivalence can never be removed. The risk for man remains, his very nature is a risk, and the issue is unpredictable.

Man's understanding of himself today is weighted by the historical decisions which he has inherited. All history is man's struggle to understand himself. But even his awareness of those decisions today is both limited and confused, so that he appears to himself now as the master, now as the slave; now as the mature and deliberate manipulator of nature and history, and now as a mere faceless number in the machinery of productivity; now as full of *Angst*, and now as an undifferentiated addition to the congealed mass of a static and meaningless agglomeration of being.

The resolution of this confusion—but not of the inherent ambivalence—depends on man's own decision. He is what he decides to be. This decision in turn depends on his understanding of his historical existence. Whether he chooses the 'holy hypochondria'[1] of his heterogeneity, and the endless restless movement of his spirit which is its expression, or whether he sinks into homogeneity, like a sick man unwilling to get better

[1]The phrase comes from a letter of J. G. Hamann to Herder, 3 June 1781. Cf. *Johann Georg Hamann, Briefwechsel* ed. W. Ziesemer and A. Henkel, Wiesbaden, 8 vols 1955*ff*.

and to brave the world again, will be determined by himself and by no extraneous powers. Samuel Beckett is right to place his characters simply in the situation of waiting;[1] even waiting without hope, 'for hope would be hope for the wrong thing'[2]. But there is a hope beyond hope of things and powers, and Beckett has scarcely done more than approach the threshold of this other dimension of hope. It is a historical hope, and it is with this that we are concerned here.

It is again Bonhoeffer who provides the impetus for man's understanding of himself in history. He speaks of man's autonomy, especially in relation to his 'discovery of the laws by which the world lives and manages in science, social and political affairs, art, ethics and religion', and while he does not wish to get involved in a discussion of the exact date of this new phenomenon, he speaks of a time 'about the thirteenth century'.[3]

It is clear that, whatever the qualifications we have to add to such an observation, there was in fact a remarkable efflorescence of man's activity which we may fairly place as succeeding the middle ages. It included the liberation from the metaphysic of the middle ages, and from the standpoint of the present day may be described as the first manifestations of what we now call secularism.[4] I take this at present, without prejudice to a fuller definition, to mean a predominantly 'this-worldly' standpoint. In its positive expression it has been characterized by Dilthey as the development of 'free manifoldness', that is, the spread of a deliberate and conscious autonomy and

---

[1] In *Waiting for Godot* Faber, London 1965, and Grove Press, New York.
[2] T. S. Eliot, *East Coker* in *Four Quartets* Faber, London 1944, and Harcourt, Brace & World Inc., New York.
[3] *op. cit.* p178.
[4] There is a useful historical survey of the word in Martin Stallmann *Was ist Säkularisierung?* J. C. B. Mohr, Tübingen 1960: it was apparently Troeltsch who first used the word in its full modern connotation.

individualizing of the interests and enterprises, both 'purely' intellectual and then more and more technological, of Renaissance and post-Renaissance man.[1] For the interest of our analysis we may note that the negative expression of this development is that modern secularist man is more and more ready to manage his life without reference to God.

But this is no more than a provisional description. It is precisely in the ambiguities of this secularism, and especially in the meaning, in this context, of the word 'God', that we have to look for clues for a right decision. Even on the basis of what has already been said here about the empirical condition of man today, it should be clear that there is an uncertainty, even a *malaise*, in the heart of 'secularism'. It is an interesting indication of this that several writers have attempted recently to distinguish between a necessary 'secularity' and a decadent or sterile 'secularism'.[2]

To grasp the full implications of what happened to man's self-understanding at the Renaissance, however, and to understand, so far as understanding is possible, why such a change took place then, it is necessary to look farther back into the story of European man than Bonhoeffer suggested. It is certainly upon the recognition by Renaissance man of his own responsibility for his history that the whole issue turns. There was undoubtedly a novel, vivid and creative recognition of man's freedom:

[1]Wilhelm Dilthey *Einleitung in die Geisteswissenschaften* Teubner, Stuttgart 1959 p356f.
[2]Cf. especially Gabriel Vahanian *The Death of God* Braziller, New York 1961 pp60ff, Friedrich Gogarten *Verhängnis und Hoffnung der Neuzeit* Stuttgart 1958, pp129ff and Rudolf Bultmann *Der Gottesgedanke und der moderne Mensch* in 'Zeitschrift für Theologie und Kirche,' December 1963, p338. English translation in *World Come of Age* (A Symposium on Dietrich Bonhoeffer) ed. R. Gregor Smith, Collins, London and Fortress Press, Philadelphia 1967, pp256ff.

no external forces, no arbitrary fate, but man himself in his deliberate assumption of responsibility for his own history, was seen, sometimes with melancholy, but more characteristically with exhilaration and even with pride, as 'the free creator of his destiny'.[1] The life of Pico della Mirandola (1463-94) is perhaps the most fascinating illustration of this audacious enterprise. It was his ambition to unite the whole of European thought in a single view of man. Though his attempt was never completed, so that we are left with little more than a legend, nevertheless in the writings he has left he is to be understood as more than an eclectic philosopher. He wanted to bring Moses and Plato, the Cabbala and the schoolmen, into subservience to Christ. His discourse *On the Dignity of Man*, intended as an introduction to the nine hundred theses with which he challenged the Church and the whole society of the learned, is more than an exercise in the glorification of man and his powers. It is the prelude to a new understanding of human history. His ideas, it is true, struck no roots at the time, and they cannot be pursued in detail here. What is of interest for our purpose, however, is that Pico, as one of the great characteristic figures of the Italian Renaissance, saw the move forward in terms of a new understanding of the past, and basically, indeed, in terms of a new understanding of Christ. The hope he had for man's future was thus derived from the hope he found in an event of the past.

We must keep this paradox in mind as we take this hint from Pico to look back into our history. And if we restrict what it is practicable to say here to the nature of biblical faith, this is

---

[1] Cf. the study of Pico by Ivan Pusino, in 'Zeitschrift für Kirchengeschichte' XLIV (1925) pp504*ff*: there is a growing interest, especially among American scholars, in Pico (cf. the essay by P. O. Kristeller in *The Renaissance Philosophy of Man*, University of Chicago Press 1948), but a full assessment is still to come.

nevertheless not intended as a restriction to any dogmatic inheritance. Rather, we wish to lengthen and enrich the perspective from which we may better assess the powers which were stirring at the Renaissance.

My basic contention can be stated briefly. The original impulse for the Renaissance and thus for the modern view of man comes from the biblical faith. The secularism of our time has its sanction in the prophetic faith. And Christ is the unreserved, unconfused, and completely consistent secularist of history. It is only on the basis of the biblical view of faith, of man and God, and in the clearest expression of this view, namely, in the life of Christ, that a real understanding and thus a radical critique of modern secularist man can be achieved.

Now clearly both the Old Testament and New Testament are a rich quarry both for theologians and for students of religious phenomena. But the biblical faith itself is in the first instance neither theology nor religion. But it is primarily history, seen simultaneously as man's actions and God's actions, but not separable from one another in their actuality. Indeed, the interaction is so complete that from the standpoint of biblical faith we may say that history is seen both as man's history and as God's history. It is the historicity of God which is the inescapable basis of the biblical view of man; and it is the historicity of man which is the only way in which God may be believed.

What the Bible provides is not theology in the sense of speculation about God. There is certainly a wealth of reflection about God, but it arises out of the context of historical action. Thus there is no questioning of the existence of God, and no effort to catalogue his attributes. The Bible is interested neither in the question of whether God exists, nor in the question of what God is in himself. But it recounts the engagement of God with men in their own history. In so doing it witnesses to the historicity of God. When the Psalmist's enemies ask him, 'Where is your God?',[1] he has no discursive argument ready to persuade them. He can only point to his faith in the movement of God in many different ways in history. What the men of the Bible bear witness to may be described as God's 'coming to speech'. And this 'speaking' consistently takes place within a situation of extreme personal engagement. The 'revelation' is not an objective account, nor an overwhelming theophany, nor a mythological structure. It is no more, and no less, than a demand laid upon a man, or a people, in and through the actual historical possibilities of the time, for which the response of faith or rejection is required in an unqualified way. What biblical faith does *not* assert is of the utmost significance.

> That God does not have a being in analogy with our being, that the Word is not a mystical experience, that faith is not an experience or any human capacity, that God cannot be conceived as a substance, nor his work as causality, and that the holy history cannot be understood as a process—all these burning and heavy-laden negations are given with the basic structure of the Bible.[2]

These negations clear the air of the Bible. Indeed, they clear the world of gods and powers. They even leave God himself out of the world. But this does not mean that the world is abandoned, or that the recognition of God in history, of the historicity of God, must be annulled. On the contrary, it is only in the paradoxical recognition of God's absence from the world that the world is freed to become what it can become, and what God wishes it to be. Only in a world which is completely de-divinized in this way is any advent of God possible. The presence of God is dialectically conjoined with his absence. In the biblical view

---

[1] e.g. Psalm 42.3 'My tears have been my food day and night, while men say to me continually, "Where is your God?".'
[2] Miskotte, *op. cit.* p23: English translation p14. (I have made my own translation.)

51

man must learn to live *etsi Deus non daretur*, as though God were not given. God not as a bit of the world, God not as an extension of the world or of man's thought about the world, God not as a monstrous imposition upon the world, but God given to the world as though he were not given; this is the rich and paradoxical summary of the biblical faith in God.

Certainly, it is this God who is 'completely other' than his people who nevertheless is with and for his people, and gives meaning to their whole history. But in the biblical faith there is no question of the reflective establishment of a doctrine either of God's transcendence or of his immanence. It is even misleading to say that in the Bible we find the definitive theological assertion of monotheism. Of course, it is true that reflections of the discursive understanding may arise on the basis of the biblical records; but they are reflections after the event. And the event itself is different; it is always *in actu*, in action, in the actual situation of the man who is called upon, required, to face his own history in terms of a present demand upon him for faith.

And what the Bible provides is not religion either, in the sense of man's search for God, and the manipulation of powers in order to reach him. Not even man's most splendid achievements can reach God, or touch him. Indeed, from the spectator's point of view the most obvious thing about the story of ancient Israel is the monotony of failure in their highest ambitions and enterprises. Yet the significance, even in the failure, is that Israel recognized that their God was nevertheless with them and for them. This is not to be understood in terms of a theodicy, as though God were apportioning the fit reward, or punishment, according to the nature of the achievement or the failure. For the people lived in and with the faith that God was active in their history. This was simply how things were: they did not need to search for God, because he was already there, and had found them. But at the same time there was no safety in this conviction, no guarantee for their historical existence.

The only assurance was in their conviction: it was *certitudo*, not *securitas*: they were utterly convinced, and at the same time launched on an unpredictable course.

It is therefore also misleading to try to isolate the element of the 'numinous' from the life of faith as the characteristic element. There is no isolation of any religious element, however described, in the history of Israel. Even if the encounter with God in history brings with it the fear of the Lord, this cannot be interpreted as the experience of a 'frisson' of the 'otherworldly', far less of the 'uncanny'. For example, when Isaiah encounters the presence of the Lord in the temple, what we are faced with in the account is the integral connexion of Isaiah's call with his historical task: 'Here am I, send me', is his response, and with these words he is launched upon a sober, even matter-of-fact, mission.

In the New Testament all these elements, the historicity, the conjunction of the presence and the absence of God, the pre-theological and the supra-religious concern, are to be found once more. But now the issue of Israel's history has narrowed down to an almost intolerable point of tension and paradox. The tension reaches its climax in the failure of the mission of Jesus, the paradox in its vindication. Here the man of faith takes the centre of the stage, and alone. Here the historical responsibility is at its purest, and most crucial. And nothing helps; nothing in the best efforts of religion. 'Jesus came into the world to destroy religion,' says Paul Tillich, and indeed the powers of the world and the efforts of man to establish a means of solving the riddle of man's being and destiny are at this point shown up as fruitless. But Tillich's dictum needs to be modified. For the efforts of men are not simply destroyed, to leave no hope. But they are conquered. In other words, even in the crucial moment of the cry of dereliction from the Cross, 'My God, my God, why hast thou forsaken me?' Jesus is not simply alone. The very invocation of God implies the recognition of God's concern.

53

Here the world is finally and conclusively emptied of hope, and cleared of would-be powers. And in this clearance the reality of the 'nevertheless' of faith comes into its own. The story of Israel reaches in the crucifixion of Jesus the point where the world is definitively released from all the powers of the world, where man is faced, in the person of Jesus, with the last decision about himself and his destiny, and is left all alone—in face of God.

This may be described as the story of man's religious yearnings, or of his theological enquiries, only in the sense that he is brought up short against their inadequacy. And here he is faced, with a unique concentration of purity and force, with the old question of what he is.

The question addressed to man at this point must not be reduced to a matter of mythological apprehensions or theological propositions about the nature of Christ. We must understand the question as carrying with it the claim that here we encounter the last Word of God. But how are we to understand this *eschaton*, this lastness, in relation to our ongoing history and especially to our normal view of religion, and to our immense modern confusion about what man really is?

An answer to this question is implicit in what has been said about biblical faith. But it is not self-evident or easy. The difficulty does not lie so much in the superficial obstacles—for example, the divided voice of the Church, or the unsurprising ambiguities of hypocrisy and self-complacency and self-righteousness and narrow-mindedness which are the constant temptations of professing Christians. For anyone who is asking with true concern what he thinks he ought to be, and how he understands the enigma of his own existence, will not be unduly influenced by the sight of the professing Christian yielding to his temptations. For he will also notice, with astonishment perhaps, the equal persistence of the man who professes to live by faith. And if he has any inkling of the nature of this faith, he will not ask for the removal of this ambiguity, but for the reason why, in spite of it, such persistence is possible at all.

From this brief look at the historical course of biblical faith we have seen that it is in the overcoming of religion, the reduction of all other gods in the world to silence, and in the concentrated pressure upon history of the God who is both absent and present, that the possibility was established for man to go his own way in a liberated world. But this possibility has never been more than dimly recognized, let alone realized. So today we are the heirs not only of this possibility in principle, but also of a confusion of images of man. We have now, in conclusion, to attempt a separation of images. The confusion might be briefly and comprehensively described as due to the failure of the Renaissance secularist insight to be worked out in a radical dialectic with the image of the new man in Christ, and in a radical conflict with the remanent images in man's consciousness.

I suggest that we may see altogether four images of what man is today. While these images are separable and distinct, they are all at home in more or less strength within each one of us.

The first image is Adam. In the mythology of the Old Testament Adam is the first man. What sort of man? Is he good, or bad? Is he what he can be, simply in the sense of becoming more and more what he is? Or is there an 'ought' in his existence which implies a break, a discontinuity, a double nature?

Adam is clearly recognized as related to God; but just as clearly he is seen as out of relation to God. He is historical man; that is, after the mythological account of the Fall has been described, he is seen as the man we still know today: broken, in a state of unrest, tension and misery. But at the same time, the grandeur of his origin is not denied, and the grandeur of his possibilities is still present to him—providing him, indeed, with nourishment for his unrest and misery. At the same time, no return is

55

possible. History is seen as irreversible; and after he is driven from the Garden of Eden, from his state of 'dreaming inno-cence', man is launched on the course of the same history as we may clearly recognize by looking into our own selves. The familiarity of the mythology should not blind us to the pene-trating power of the analysis. We are all this Adam, and we are all heirs simultaneously of his grandeur and his misery:

> *The whole earth is our hospital*
> *Endowed by the ruined millionaire,*
> *Wherein, if we do well, we shall*
> *Die of the absolute paternal care*
> *That will not leave us, but prevents us everywhere.*[1]

But the answer to which Mr Eliot has already alluded in these lines, by speaking of the incessant 'paternal care' which is to cure us by a death of the sickness of Adam, is not a matter of course. Are we to interpret the cure as being a matter of religion? The image of *homo religiosus*, religious man, is the second of the images that in some form is discernible in us all. This has indeed traditionally been the favourite image for man when he is driven to despair in the Adam he finds in himself. And it is still very much alive in modern man, as it was alive in the time of the Renaissance. Even if we agree with Bonhoeffer that the age of religion is past, it is only in a limited sense that this is true. The age which accepted man's destiny as being determined within a metaphysical frame of the natural and the supernatural, with his salvation assured by his proper adherence to an authority of grace regarded as seizing him with arbitrary power—that age is certainly past. So too is the age of individualist religion and piety, whatever the rearguard actions which may be fought on behalf of what is a peculiarly Protestant heterodoxy. But if we

[1]T. S. Eliot, *East Coker*, in *Four Quartets*, Faber, London 1944, and Harcourt, Brace & World Inc., New York.

understand religion in the sense of the Bible—in the sense, that is, to which the biblical faith is so consistently hostile—and more generally as we see it at work in the non-biblical religions, as the means of building up the powers of man in order to establish with God a relation which is already potentially present in man —in a religious *a priori* or a basic identity of man's being with God, or the like—then this type of religion is by no means past. It may be found within the styles of life and worship encouraged by the churches, but it may also be seen outside official Christianity. Certainly, it takes very different and very varied forms outside the life of the churches, and the name of God has mostly been suppressed. This silence about God, however, is a more honest indication of this kind of religiousness than the calling upon his name at the wrong address. But whether this form of religion is officially within the churches, or whether it is outside, in the form of adherence to some ideology, the basic feature is the same: it is the worship of some bit of the world, masquerading as absolute, and it does not matter whether this takes the form of some 'secularist' faith (such as certain brands of so-called scientific humanism, or nationalism, or aestheticism, or moralism) or of one of the current variations of Christianity. What we are faced with, in each instance, is the basic characteristic of the second image, namely, the build-up of assurances within the world in order to secure man from the icy blast of the still unanswered question, Who then am I? The image of the religious man, however attractive at times to us all, and whether it is expressed in the styles of modern scientism or in the old-fashioned forms of dogmatic Christianity, is unable to penetrate beyond the world of objects.

Religion can indeed take many forms. Thus even modern secularism can illustrate the persistence and the ubiquity of the religious short-circuiting of the question of man. The greatest problem which faces the candid secularist today, who has learned something of the lesson of the Renaissance, is how he is to avoid ending in the prison of his own self. If it is true that the religious man (as distinct from the man of faith) simply makes a detour over symbols that pretend to aim at God, and returns to his own self,[1] so too the secular man of today, while he may avoid the particular pretence of turning to God, nevertheless returns only too easily to himself. He wanders in a no-man's land in which no-man, nemo, is the only reflection he sees when he looks within himself, or outside himself. The terror of an infinite regress of mirrors is the nightmare of modern secularist man's self-exploration. So he tries to justify his self-understanding by abstractions about the future of man, or the preservation of civilization, or happiness, or even by asserting the virtue of innovation for its own sake. This secularist man, who is the third image of man in all of us today, in more or less clarity of outline, desires to have an eschatology which is like Melchizedek in the Bible, without any genealogy, suddenly appearing on the scene of history, without beginning and without end. This can only mean that secularist man of this type, when this particular image gains the ascendancy in his life, is turned in on himself in the most calamitous self-despair or an even more ominous self-esteem. The religion associated with the old Gnostic mythology regarded this world as a prison from which the soul longed to be released. But the unradical secularism of our time desires to make a virtue out of what appears to it to be the necessity of man's complete and absolute imprisonment in his own self.

But to choose oneself in this way means the negation of man's real dialectic with his own history. It is not basic liberation, but basic slavery. It is, incidentally, an abrogation of the historical concern which is so splendidly exemplified at the Renaissance.

The historical hope, which is the *motif* of this analysis, lies in

---

[1] Cf. L. Ziegler *Magna Charta* 1923, quoted in Miskotte *op. cit.* p12: English translation p3.

the fourth image. By this I mean the biblical image which is adumbrated in the prophetic faith and present to faith in the person, or the event, of Christ. He is, as St Paul says, 'the last Adam', or 'the second man'.[1] He is, to faith, the new historical possibility of man; he is the invitation to man, supplying both the question and the possibility of the answer regarding what man is. He is, to faith, what man can be, and what God wants man to be. He is man's history and God's history in one.

This is not the place for a survey of the whole range of theological statements about Christ. What is important for our purpose is to recognize the power that is present in the open facing of the image of this man. To this end I restrict myself to a few observations.

First, the image of Christ as the 'last' man, or as the eschatological event, does not imply that by historical research we may be able to construct a picture of Jesus, guaranteed authentic, and carrying with it, as a self-evident 'fact' of history, the claim to present a static, ascertainable, and demonstrable truth about the ultimate nature of man. This kind of reconstruction, even if it were possible, would not be the living historical and eschatological event which is the heart of the Christian message, and the source of Christian faith. But it would be at best an archaist image, outside the real dynamic of history.

Second, the image of Christ as the eschatological man is not to be understood as reposing in past history. What is available to us of this image by the attentive and expectant listening to what we may hear from the biblical accounts is not the wholeness of this image. For it comes to us in the broken and ambiguous forms of history, and of our own history. If the appeal of Christianity were to be isolated to the objectified and necessarily mythological picture which is available to us through the forms and structures of history, then Christianity would indeed long

[1] I Corinthians 15. 45 and 47

ago have succumbed to the legendary and superstitious trappings with which it has again and again been embellished. But the image is available in the form of a claim upon us in our present being, in our present historical situation.

But third, the image of Christ as the last and decisive event of man's history is not just an encouragement to each man who has faith, as a means of withstanding, and maintaining hope in his present situation. But it is also an opening up of the future. It is the constant re-opening of the present, pointing to ever new possibilities. In this sense the image of Christ is never complete, in the whole course of human history. It is always ahead of us, inviting us to newness. It is able to do this just because it is *the* paradoxical event of human history in which man is challenged, and given the means, to establish a radical critique of all the other images. This is the only image for man which gives up hope in any powers of the world, and at the same time points man back to his responsibility for himself and his world.

The movement of the spirit of man which is thus established in history may be seen high-lighted in the Renaissance; but in contrast with the possibilities inherent in this image, the Renaissance is no more than a gleam in the dark.

It is in this perspective that the modified secularism which is characteristic of our time has to be judged as being not radical enough. Only a Christian secularity, to use Vahanian's term, is radical enough. That is to say, only a view of man which is both absolutely free, and absolutely responsible, is able to confront the dizzy prospect of our time—not, indeed, with equanimity, but with a reasonable hope. For only the radicality of the hopelessness of man's condition, with the simultaneous radicality of the new hope which he is given, as these are to be encountered, conjoined, in the single image of Christ as the man who in his being finalizes the reality of God's historical care—only this twofold radicality is able to carry man through the deep-going antinomies of his existence.

The ambiguities, however, cannot be removed. The incessant slide of man's freedom into bondage or into licence, the despair which is the other side of his hope, the threat of *nihil* which rushes in on him from each side of the narrow way, are a necessary part of his destiny.

In this sense the secondary images of the religious man and of the short-term secularist, as well as the image of Adam, will always be with him. So far as the image of 'religious man' is concerned, we are not simply 'justified' by the Last Man, but (as Luther saw so clearly) we also remain sinners. And so far as the modified secularism of our time is concerned, we are never freed in the sense of being given our freedom as an absolute possession. For this could only confirm us in the despair of self-possession. And so far as the image of Adam is concerned, this must remain so long as we recognize our basic historical finitude and relativity. But in and through the recognition of these historical images, man is able to deal with them. He is able to do so if he recognizes simultaneously what is happening to him both as thoroughly historical and as of another order from the rest of his historical self-understanding. It is thoroughly historical in that it is grounded in a historical life which is engaged in a realistic conflict with all the other historical images of man. And it is of another order from these in that it is simultaneously given to man as the final movement of God into history. In being encouraged by the central force of the Christian tradition to hold fast to this dominant image, the man of faith, in the unrest of his faith, finds that he is being held fast. And if we call this paradoxical experience man's final struggle for self-understanding, and the nearest to fullness of self-understanding that is given to him in history, then it must also be clearly affirmed that this struggle, when carried to the utmost in the depths of a faith and a hope in man and his history that simply will not let go, turns out to involve a gift. We are given the chance, the choice, to choose ourselves in this way. But if we make this choice of faith, that is, in the context of confrontation by the last image of man, then we will find that in truth we have not chosen ourselves, but we have been chosen.

This is the basic liberation of man. But it is a liberation into and for history. So in the strength of this basic liberation the other historical images still have a place, but they no longer have ultimate power. Adam, the religious man, and the free but lost secularist of our time, are always with us, and in us; but they are in principle overcome.

IV

Humanism and the Church in Deadlock

In speaking of post-renaissance man, I ended by speaking of man's basic liberation into history and for history. From the standpoint of Christianity we can see the Renaissance as providing for it an opportunity not only to free itself from the bonds of a dualist metaphysics but also to enter on a new course in relation to its understanding of God and of the world and of man's historical destiny. In the outflow of spiritual and intellectual and physical energy into a truly breath-taking variety of enterprises, it was possible, and for a time seemed probable, that at the centre of this outreaching of the human spirit the energy of Christianity would be the corrective and shaping element, guiding the autonomous enterprises, penetrating them, and in turn being penetrated by them. It seemed as though it were indeed possible for a new kind of civilization to arise, which could develop, in unheard-of depth and grandeur, what Professor Tillich would call a theonomous life. By a theonomy Tillich means, to use his own words, a 'culture expressing in its creations an ultimate concern and a transcending meaning not as something strange but as its own spiritual ground. "Religion is the substance of culture and culture the form of religion".'[1]

But this possibility has not so far been fulfilled. What happened, in the confusion of interests and possibilities which succeeded the break-up of the mediaeval heteronomous culture

[1]Paul Tillich *The Protestant Era* Nisbet, Welwyn 1951, p36.

was that—speaking in broad outline—the Church and civilization went separate ways. Western society broke up not only into a great number of more or less independent nation-states, with almost unlimited ambitions of self-assertion and self-aggrandizement; but its cultural interests also developed in a multitude of independent ways. These ambitions and interests were based on a conception of the unfettered autonomous human spirit of exploration and enquiry which was bound by nothing save the consideration of the 'given facts'. Human life was seen as an autonomous entity, which could be understood and controlled in terms of principles derived not from outside itself but always from within its own history. To quote Tillich again 'autonomy is the dynamic principle of history . . . (it) is not nekessarily a turning-away from the unconditional. It is, so to speak, the obedient acceptance of the unconditional character of the form, the logos, the universal reason in world and mind. It is the acceptance of the norms of truth and justice, of order and beauty, of personality and community. It is obedience to the principles that control the realms of individual and social culture.'[1] The old categories of body and spirit, nature and super-nature, profane and sacred, no longer played the chief controlling part. These categories were derived from the metaphysical heteronomy of the late Middle Ages, and gave way before the category of history as 'the outstanding category of interpreting reality'.[2] In this new historical autonomy the distinguishing categories were found within the integral life of man, that is, man's life seen as a single whole, an independent entity. The divisions now run through man and his history and no longer through man and God, earth and heaven. From this new maturity of man in history there have flowed all the characteristically modern developments: historical science, archaeology, economics, politics, psychology, sociology, and the

[1] *op. cit.* p52.
[2] *op. cit.* p30.

natural sciences—all resting, whatever their differences and even conflicts of interest, on the same ground of man's nature regarded as an autonomous entity. The fruits of this maturity have been exhilarating as well as frightening. But our present fears should not blind us to the immense gains which have thereby been made available for western civilization, and through it for the whole world. As Cyprian said of the Church during the decay of the Roman empire that 'it stands upright among the ruins', so we must also acknowledge that in the ruins of the great Christian experiment of the Middle Ages, man himself stood upright, and took over his own rule without fear.

Against this autonomous development, this conception, commonly called secular, of man and his destiny, the Church reacted slowly but powerfully and in the end without many signs of regret or attempt at conciliation. While the activist humanist Renaissance gradually developed its resources, opening up one field after another to its open-minded curiosity about the 'facts', the Church drew slowly back within itself, re-iterating what seemed to it to be the 'essential facts'. The situation was not essentially different in the Protestant churches and in the rump of the old Church, though on the whole the Protestant churches have in the course of these centuries shown more clearly both their close affinity to and appreciation of the new civilization of autonomous humanism and the violence of reaction against it. The Roman Catholic too, however, has in recent times, particularly since Vatican II, been drawn into the same tension of appreciation and violent discussion. In the basic Christian tradition, therefore, we recognize the same struggle. There are both conflicts and attempts at accommodation, as one strongpoint after another is attacked by the spirit of autonomous man. The prolonged and bitter controversy in the eighteenth century between the *illuminati* and the evangelical party in England, which was mostly regarded as a quarrel about the evidence of the gospel miracles for the truth of Christianity, was in fact one of the crucial points at which the Church's conception of the authority of revelation had to yield before the onslaught of the conception of autonomous human reason. In this conflict David Hume played a conspicuous part whose importance has been increasingly recognized. Nothing less than two ways of understanding human existence came into conflict, and in the sharpness of that controversy and its succeeding phases in the nineteenth and twentieth centuries, the separation of ways became increasingly clear.

The conflict affected both sides, but it has been, I believe, the Church which has suffered most. For the perennial temptation of every religion, which seeks to understand and explain human life in terms of some unconditional ground, is to short-circuit the principles controlling the individual and society by means of principles of understanding and explanation brought in from outside human life itself: some secure foothold from which it may survey mankind, offering men consolation and assurance, indeed, but at the same time making it a condition of that offer that it itself, the religion, should be accepted along with these gifts, as the purveyor of them. The Church, following this temptation, has more and more, in recent centuries, sharpened and strengthened its understanding of its message conceived as a separate instrument of power. It has attempted to contrive for itself, out of the fragments of the whole tradition of Christian authority, a new heteronomous structure. The orthodox elaboration of creeds, confessions, catechisms, liturgies and rituals—and now, in our time, of a new insistence on what is called biblical theology—may be summarily described as a series of attempts to build up a structure of authority to replace the broken tradition of the mediaeval Church. But all this effort betrays a fundamental difference from the early history of the Church. Then the fundamental concern was to express—through the exigencies of conflict with heretics and unbelievers, certainly, but still, simply to express—unconditional concern for the historical needs of men. Since the coming of age of man in society, however, the fundamental concern has changed: the Church has sought to *preserve* its message, and with the message to preserve itself. It has sought to do this by imposing itself and its message as an alien law on man's mind. It has sought to define this task, and its whole situation vis-à-vis society, in terms of delimitation of interests. Then it has proceeded to aim at exercising power on society by the establishment of its heteronomous authority.

Let me pause a moment, to make clear what I mean by this word: following Tillich's fruitful terminology, I mean by a heteronomy a system of ideas, or a structure of laws, which seek to impose themselves on the forms of a society to which they are fundamentally alien. Heteronomy 'disregards the logos structure of mind and world. It destroys the honesty of truth and the dignity of the moral personality. It undermines creativity and the humanity of man. Its symbol is the "terror" exercised by absolute churches or absolute states.'[1] A very good example of a heteronomous church and state in unholy alliance was the action of the magistrates of Edinburgh for some time during the eighteenth century. Acting on the advice of the presbytery of the church, the magistrates appointed two baillies or bailiffs to parade the streets of Edinburgh during the hours of church service, with power to arrest and fine any citizens who were found promenading instead of being in church. But there are many examples, for which we do not really need to cast back into other centuries. A heteronomous authority, especially a church, is not willing to allow the world to be itself, not even when that world is a mature world with its own forms and purposes, not even when that world has derived its fundamental

[1]*op. cit.* p52.

impulse and its historical self-understanding from the very heart and substance of Christian faith itself—as our modern world has done. This heteronomous effort reaches a typical climax in the modern orthodoxy or neo-orthodoxy known variously as the theology of crisis, dialectical theology, or the theology of the Word. I scarcely need to point out that in making this criticism I am not decrying the magnificent power and splendour of some of the manifestations of neo-orthodoxy: the concern for the *kerygma*, or essential message of the gospel, the attention to the actual history and theology of the Bible, the devotion, even the passion, with which the omnipotence and judgement of God are proclaimed over against all human confusion and distortion of revelation. Nevertheless, the question which we have to ask is whether the Church is really fulfilling in this way the fundamental concern for man and his history which is the reason for its existence. 'The Word of God is not a word spoken only to the ears, or even necessarily to the ears at all. The Word of God is his self-communication which can occur in many forms and is not bound to the human word. It may occur through actions, gestures, forms—of course, not *ex opere operato* (by their mere performance), but nevertheless without any accompanying word. Sacraments, visible symbols, bodily, musical, artistic expressions are "Word of God" even if nothing is spoken—that is, for those who accept them spiritually (as the spoken word is Word of God *only* if it is received spiritually).'[1]

We might go farther than Tillich in this, and ask whether a Church which has even such a wide and generous understanding of the context and utterance of the Word of God has found the proper relation to human life and society. For in the end the Church in its fundamental concern should not be living in a different world from the rest of men. It does not stand outside this world, it is not in heaven, it does not even carry the respon-

---

[1]Tillich *op. cit.* p218.

sibility for heaven, that is, for God's place and power. The work which the Church does truly for God it does by being truly for men, with men, and it does this work through men. This conception of the Church's task cuts from underneath it all supposed security, all sacrosanct authority, all search for a lever of power on the world, all heteronomous ambitions. The Word of God may then be seen as being spoken in ever new forms which are created out of the experiences and enterprises of men in the actual situations where they are.

But though the divergence is violent and sharp between the life of autonomous secularized man and the would-be heteronomous life of the Church, the fundamental concern of both parties is the same: it is the life of man. The lesson I draw from the struggle of recent centuries is that neither party is complete without the other. The free exercise of the human spirit in the autonomous consideration of the objects presented to it is legitimate and right; man's relation to the objects in his world, to his own history, does contain unconditional validity. But this validity is not complete without the recognition of certain inescapable boundaries which lie across its path. And on the other hand the obedient devotion of the human spirit to the objects of Christian revelation is not complete without the recognition of the freedom of the human spirit. The recognition of the need for obedience to bounds in the one case does not damage freedom, and the recognition of freedom in the other case does not damage obedience. The unsolved mediaeval controversy about the freedom or predestination of the will cannot be solved either by the heteronomous assertions of the post-mediaeval churches or by the autonomous defiance of a sterile and secondary humanism. To cling to either side of the controversy as giving the solution to the human predicament really means to cling to one side or the other of a metaphysical misunderstanding.

Both sides, I repeat, have in common the situation of man in history, in this one world. The struggle is round man himself, and an understanding of what he is. What we are concerned with, therefore, is the search for a new anthropology, a view of man, which will pay proper respect both to the insights of the Renaissance about man and the insights of Christianity about God in relation to man. In this search I do not believe that it can be fruitful, or even legitimate, to attempt to take our stand on the old battle-fields, where the corpses of decaying categories are locked in meaningless embrace, where revelation lies stricken beside reason, where the supernatural lies dead beside the natural, where the trumpet of the Lord, borrowed by the dying dogmatist, lies tarnished by the side of the deaf and also dying secular hero, captain of his fate no longer. The knight of faith, as Kierkegaard called him in a beautiful image, can no longer come prancing into the tournament in the panoply of absolute assurance. Absolute solicitude, yes; and absolute resignation. For he comes not from another world but in the new hope and strength which he is given in this world because of what has been done in and for this world. Like his master, he is the servant, so far as he may be, of men.

In the historical situation of man, then, it is necessary to recognize that freedom and obedience both have their place. The human spirit is free so far as it knows no limits within itself to the possibilities which it may unfold. And the human spirit is at the same time bound to strict obedience to the facts out of which these possibilities flow. These facts are the given objects, the things and people, by which it tests and develops its freedom. Everything that man undertakes he does so in virtue of the things and people coming towards him from outside himself. He did not make them, he did not think of them, he did not ask for them: they are there, in their own right of existence. Man is made by his free acceptance, in unlimited openness, of what comes to him out of the surrounding darkness.

And likewise the Christian, though bound by his special facts, what he calls the 'facts of the revelation', and thus also, formally speaking, bound by what comes from outside himself, by what he neither invented nor imagined, is at the same time invited into a realm of freedom. Admittedly, if we limit our gaze simply to the historical manifestations of Christianity, we are at once involved in all manner of fateful and even baleful circumscriptions of this realm of freedom. Throughout its history the Church has struggled with the invitation to freedom as though it were an incubus of which it would like to be rid. Authority, and expediency, and the exercise of power by virtue of certain semi-magical delimitations of influence, have all played an insidious part in diverting the energy of Christendom from its proper sphere. The doctrine of the Holy Spirit in an integral unity with a full doctrine of the Word has always been the laggard in the armoury of Christianity. For it is in this teaching that the explosive and revolutionary quality of Christianity is seen at its most potent: the teaching, namely, which affirms man and his history as leading through grace into unimagined spheres of truth and freedom. The generally neglected teaching about freedom which lies at the very heart of Christianity is an affirmation of man's infinite possibilities.

For it is in a proper grasp of the life of the Spirit as actually constituting the community of Christians that the ancient energies of Christianity may be rediscovered. Though the tragic course of one of the first great movements of the Spirit in the life of the Church—the Montanist movement, which included in its story the life of Tertullian, one of the truly original thinkers of the Church—can scarcely now be seen as anything but inevitable, nevertheless, it must be said that here as elsewhere the Church has ever been quick to protect its gains, to retain its status as an authority in the world, and slow to see the dialectic in its obedience to its own calling. For this calling is not to a *position* in the world, but to a disclosure of the dialectic in man's own being, in the heart of history: a dialectic which de-

mands freedom as well as obedience, absolute openness, unreserved togetherness with others, as the very place where the
Spirit is present. God's presence is thus not a shadowy longing
in the life of the Church, but the very being of Christianity in
the world. Living with this presence cannot be guaranteed in
any due observance of the Church's forms, or recognition of its
authority, but is to be awaited wherever men find themselves
brought together in some common purpose. The Church as a
sociological entity has no monopoly or guarantee of the presence of the Spirit, but is on the contrary by its very nature as an
established social institution in constant peril of losing the
Spirit.

It is a feeble and insufficient recognition of the newness of the
Incarnation as a given fact of the human situation which has
led the Church into its recoil from the Renaissance. And it is
the consequent reaction of the humanists which has sharpened
the division to the point of tragedy. It is not too much to say
that until this tragic division has been overcome the modern
world is going to find no way through its deadlock.

For on the one hand, among the unchurched humanists,
though truth has been the guiding star, the recognition of
bounds has faded. And on the other hand in the Church,
though being has been the explicit goal, this has been sought in
the strength of a false spirituality, what Kierkegaard called religiosity, and the search for truth has been broken off. The greatest achievements of modern Christianity have been in the
realm of individualism, of private religion, of pietism, while
community, being together, has practically disappeared. And
with this loss of community individualism has replaced true
being in the life of the Church, and has ousted the hope of a
proper ontology and ground for community. In recent centuries all the dangers of an unbounded search for truth, or an
unbounded pursuit of being, each in separation from the other,
has characterized the two parties, the humanist and the church

parties. There has been an almost complete disregard of the disintegrating community which belongs to neither side of the ideological conflict, but to man, the battleground. Individualism, romanticism, subjectivism, antinomianism, licence of one kind or another, on the Christian or the humanist side, have been the accepted situation. On the Christian side these things have taken the form of sectarian or fissiparous tendencies, or the arrogant individualism of devotion to the inner light, or convulsive revivalism increasingly losing its contact with the forms of the given objects of the faith, and depending on a whipped-up concentrate of mock and archaic being—in brief, we see the loss of the object, of true transcendence, in a vain effort to achieve conversion by one's own inward powers of being. On the humanist side the devotion to the truth of the object, without a corresponding recognition of the bounds imposed by the proper being of the object in community, that is, in its relationships with the rest of the world, has led to more and more frantic acquisition of objects of truth in separated meaninglessness. The scientists who today represent in the common view the vanguard of human enterprise are lost in a desert, each in his own desert of truth.

The two sides share the one failure, the failure to recognize the union of freedom with bounds, of facts with relationships. This failure is focused in the failure to understand man himself. The Christians are lost in devotion to a false and separated Thou, not the great eternal Thou of given transcendence: and the humanists are lost in a false and separated It, not the living It by which man is able to reach the Thou, the It which may become a Thou. This is a failure in self-understanding, and the collapse of Christianity and humanism alike.

A new approach is needed: the combination of the situation with the relation, of what we are with what faces us. It is the problem of the nature of the object, the nature of the relation, and the meaning of transcendence.

73

The problem is not insoluble. But a prerequisite for its solution is the confession of the Church, on the one hand, that it has too long regarded the sphere of history as one which it is called to govern and control, and the readiness of the adult mature world, on the other hand, to perceive the ground of its work and hope in the same history, a history which carries with it unconditional validity.

The mysterious and crucial and unconditional moment in that history is still that point where the Christian affirmation about Christ is to be encountered. But in order to let this point of human history be effective in its own radiance it is necessary not to confuse it with the heteronomous ecclesiastical doctrines about it, or with the sterile relativisms of unbridled humanism. The crucial problem for human life and thought is the problem of transcendence. This is not an academic problem, it is not confined to metaphysical speculation about the limits of human thought and what lies beyond these limits. But the problem has been set by the Christian affirmation of the Incarnation in the midst of human life, the same life which is shared by the Christian and the non-Christian.

And when I say that the problem of transcendence is in the midst of human life I am demanding from the humanist and the Christian alike the recognition of something that is not in the first instance a matter of faith, and therefore a matter of response to a given message about Christ, but simply a matter of sight, of everyday experience. I mean, that in every human situation there is a relation: a relation between the tool and the user of the tool, between the object under investigation and the investigator, between yourself and the other person with whom you have to do. Life is characterized by these relations. Above all in the relation between two persons it becomes clear that the relation is only possible because there is a difference. It is the otherness of the other which rises up before you, in conflict or in understanding. This is the basic manifestation of transcendence in human life. This is what faces you in every situation into which you enter without reserve or reduction. This otherness or transcendence is not an extra brought in from some remote sphere of understanding, but it is the central element which makes the situation, that is, the relation, the humanity of life, possible at all. An absolute solitary is not a human being.

To put the matter sharply, as sharply as possible, in terms of modern Christian dogmatics, I believe that it is meaningless to assert, over against the secularized world, that the God of the Christians is 'wholly other'. The importance of the intention behind this assertion is clear: it is the attempt to give God his glory, to preserve his otherness, to indicate his absolute difference from his creation. But it is meaningless, because an assertion about the 'wholly otherness' by its own definition excludes any relation or knowledge of what is *wholly* other. And this assertion, besides being meaningless, distorts the sense and drift of Christianity. For the otherness which we meet in God is that otherness which we are able to meet only because he has made himself present to us, has brought himself into relation with us, in all the variety of the historical situations in which each one of us is set. We know God as transcendent because we meet him as the one who fills our present. We believe him because we know him in these situations. We believe him because he has made himself known to us in history, in humanity, in Israel, and especially in the life situation of one man, in the Incarnation.

In sum, we believe in God because we meet him in the midst of history. God is not at the end of our enquiries, nor is he the stop-gap where our thoughts fail us. To treat him in this way is to betray a fundamental disbelief both in his work as Creator and his work as Redeemer. The God of Christian belief is not a *deus ex machina* who can be called in, in the name of an otherworldly hope beyond all appearances, a god whose real home is up in the clouds, or in the wings of the theatre where man's little drama is being played out. But he is in the midst of the drama, which turns out, in consequence, to be no mere spectacle, but the real thing. We are driven to this conclusion by the very affirmation of man's life and being which is presented to us in that crucial moment of human history, the Incarnation.

On this view the beginning of a new *rapprochement* between the world and the Church depends primarily on the Church's fresh understanding of its commission and its situation. The Church is not called to be the governess of a child under age, or the warder of a condemned world. But Christians are rather placed under a double allegiance, an allegiance to the world, and an allegiance to God. In actual living history, however, this allegiance is not two things, but two sides of the one thing. For Christians in this regard as in every other cannot be more than their master, whose relation to God was lived out in his relation to the world. Christ is not a heavenly fantasy, or a *tour de force* on the part of an inaccessible otherness; but he is the givenness of transcendence, he is transcendence in its only accessible form, namely, in a human life in human history, in the one world which all men share as the place of their destiny.

If this recognition were really existential in the Church, then a great deal of contemporary ecclesiastical effort, as well as a great deal of professional gloom and even despair among church people, could be diverted into other channels. I cannot, for instance, believe that the great ecumenical movement among the non-Roman churches will move out of its present impasse —in which a due recognition of differences is having the unfortunate effect of leading to an intensification rather than amelioration of those differences—until a profound effort is made to recognize both the need and the proper claims of the so-called secular humanist world. Towards the need of that world the Church has no other task than it has always had—to serve. And towards the claims of the world the Church is required to pay much more attentive respect than hitherto. What

I am thinking of here is a temper as well as a quality of mind, rather than new set of principles: a temper and a quality of mind which will allow the world to be itself and in loving humility to elicit from the world's achievements and from its failures the possibilities which might lead it farther. What is required is what Jacques Ellul calls a 'style of life'. The Church cannot stand over the world with a whip; nor can it get behind it with a load of dynamite. The whip and the dynamite, where available, would be better used on itself. The world is not, I think, 'hungry for God' in the sense of popular conservatizing evangelists, who really mean by that a hunger to hear their own words in the old accepted terminology of their fathers—or rather their grandfathers (for their fathers knew better). The world is very suspicious, and rightly so, of those who cry 'The temple of the Lord are these', for it has had long experience of the unbridled ambitions of the Church over against the world. What the world would really see gladly is an honest and complete recognition, without any ulterior motives, by those who claim to carry forward the message of Christianity, of the existence of the world with all its own principles of movement, hopes and possibilities.

If I may venture a specific criticism, I should say that the Church needs not only in its practice but above all in its spiritual and intellectual pursuits in its colleges and universities, as well as in the manses and vicarages of its clergy, to be able far more thoroughly to identify itself, without reserve, with the studies and work of the world. It needs to recognize the hidden unconditional ground even in the most autonomous of human pursuits, it needs to welcome those pursuits not for the hope that they may be violently 'baptized' into Christ, but for their own sake. I would rather see more Christians devoting themselves today to some pursuit in what is commonly called the world—whether an intellectual study or a practical activity—than an increase in the numbers of theological students, however desirable that may seem for the immediate purposes and needs of the church authorities. If the unity of truth and being in Christ is more than a piece of sentimentalizing, then this identifying of oneself fully with the things and the people in the world is in fact an absolutely necessary step in the same direction taken by the incarnate Lord, who took upon himself the form of a servant in absolute seriousness and not merely as a docetic whimsy.

V
Towards a New Humanism

So far I have been content to give a historical survey and a cultural analysis of the problem which lies at the heart of Christian history, the problem which obsessed Kierkegaard and which can be summed up in his persistent question, 'How do I become a Christian?' I have shown how the Church, though it has tried different ways and faced several critical moments, did not follow out the possibilities which were opened up with the break-up of the mediaeval metaphysical domination. Today, in the midst of a world characterized by anxiety and hopelessness, we are still asking, and being asked, the same question. We are in the midst of a crisis in human history of unprecedented dimensions. How is the fundamental question, the question about God and Christ and our relation to them, being answered?

In general, I think it is true to say that the acuteness of the crisis, with its long roots back into Christian history, has not been recognized by any of the conventional groups within the Church. The assumptions made by these groups are too abstract; or they are mere clichés; or they cling grimly to some part of the truth, or some expression of it, which was once, in its own time and place, urgent and operative for history, but is now a museum piece, shabby and out-moded, because unable to work, unable to catch and fire the imagination and the will as well as the uneasy conscience and faltering understanding of men today.

I want first, therefore, to look at some of these main groupings or tendencies in the Church, and examine their relation to the present questions of men, as well as their provenance in history. The first main tendency I should describe as archaism. This may take one of several different forms, but in general it is characterized by a kind of nostalgia for some great figure or event in the history of the group. For example, neo-Thomism, a reiteration and re-furbishing of the dogmatic structure of St Thomas Aquinas, is sometimes claimed as the panacea for the problems of society. With the aid of a philosophy which was formulated in quite different conditions and for quite different ends, the adherents of this archaism attempt to interpret the nature and the predicament of man in this twentieth century. In contrast with the shifting and uncertain claims of other groups, the neo-Thomist movement is a mighty authority. I do not need to elaborate this by detailing its conquests of individual minds. An interesting sociological study could be made of the particular kinds of people who are attracted in their adult life into the Roman communion. Undoubtedly the aesthetic grandeur of the Roman tradition is attractive, while in recent times it has more and more blurred, or even attempted to delete, the harsh lines of authoritarian dogma. Again, the plausible and impressive philosophy of the analogy of being serves to soften the rigid lines of thought. And thirdly, it is important to remember that the Roman Church is almost as much an ideal or a grandiose accommodating and comprehensive symbol, open and generous to all kinds of temperaments and ideas, as it is an aesthetic tradition and a dogmatic system. Its outlines may therefore easily be blurred, or may appear so remote to the individual, that he may move comfortably within the allotted space. But the space *is* an allotted one, as can well appear with sudden clarity and sharpness in any emergency of belief or of morals. The *ex cathedra* pronouncements of the papal authority in these realms are the waiting dragon to encircle and devour any overreaching freedom of the human spirit.

It is true that the spirit of *aggiornimento* is there; and perhaps nothing can be the same for the Roman Catholic Church since Vatican II. It is even possible that the authoritarian claim, which has been the distinctive feature, to the outsider, since the Council of Trent will be interpreted in such a way that the Protestant churches will be left behind, submerged in domestic conflicts about their standards and confessions.

However that may be, it is essential to realize that any heteronomous authority which is set up over men's lives is in the last resort a denial of the real independence of men, their responsibility for their own destiny, and their freedom to give substance to their destiny in ever new forms of society and thought. By such a backward spring into history men are indeed invited to find rest for their minds; and within the generous confines set by the worldly authority of an authoritarian church many people do indeed find rest, and strength to achieve what they may achieve in such circumstances. But not all the grandeur and success of this movement can make up for the loss of the essential freedom of the human spirit, without which in the end the human spirit must stifle. Out of the fixed transcendent categories of Thomism, grandiose, substantial, and eternal, there flows no quickening spirit for the needs and problems of our time. Only by turning on our traces, only by being blind and deaf to the cries and questions of our fellow-men today, is it possible to imagine that we have found the absolute solution for the world in such a retrogression.

The archaism of neo-Calvinism does not have anything essentially different to offer. It too turns in romantic longing back to the great figure of its past. Its note has perhaps less of grand tragedy in it than the resolute and sustained effort of the Old Church. For though the same cardinal principle of heteronomy is at work here too—the principle, that is, of imposing an alien dogmatic system on a society which is looking in entirely different directions—the Calvinist heteronomy is no more than

81

a shadow of the great dogmatic system of the mediaeval Church. In its deepest impulses the Reformation was never intended to mean the re-establishment of the old authority in new dress. When Luther cast aside 'holy clothes' he was doing more than divest himself of the trappings of a corrupt authority: he was acting under the impulse of that movement of the human spirit which I have called the great revolution in man's self-understanding. To attempt to identify this movement of the spirit, as neo-Calvinism does, even with a purified form of the heteronomous institution of the Church, is a fearful mutilation of the emergent new society. For it was no new dogma, not even *sola fide*, considered as a dogma of the old kind, which was the real characteristic of the Reformation. The Protestant spirit needs to be characterized rather in terms of a living encounter with the Holy Spirit, with responsibility and freedom towards and in history. Of this positive side of things I shall have more to say in the next chapter.

Another grouping may be seen today on a different basis, a narrower front, within the opposed battalions of the Church itself. This is the now well-established conflict between fundamentalism and liberalism. This has so many variations, and has now gone on for so long, that it might almost seem to be a necessity for the existence of the Church—like the battles in George Orwell's story, *Nineteen Eighty-four*, where wars went on between the great configurations of forces as a matter of policy and a matter of course. The battle within the Church circles round a very important question—namely, the question of the method by which Christian truth is expressed, handed down, and to be preached. More precisely, the question is about the authority of the Scriptures, of the Old and New Testaments. The fundamentalist view clings to the doctrine of the verbal inerrancy of the whole body of Scripture. This doctrine is, of the two, the more complete and immediately satisfying. For it makes an uncompromising demand for the sacrifice of the whole spirit of intellectual enquiry. This demand is disguised as the claim of the very Word of God upon your mind, and is mostly taken, by opponents as well as adherents, at the value it puts upon itself. In other words, if you are prepared to deliver your mind, shackled and submissive, to the claims of the Word as a vast and efficient juggernaut, then here too you are promised peace of a kind. You may even find this peace. But behind the disguise of a total submission to the Word of God there lurks in fact another man-made structure, namely, a highly selective theory of revelation, a kind of gnosticism which claims to drag down from heaven an individual experience of illumination sufficient for every situation and problem which may arise in human conduct and aspiration at any period. In this selective appropriation of 'knowledge' necessary for salvation there is implicit an absolute denial of the whole movement of the human spirit which you find displayed in such a character as Petrarch, or Francis Bacon, or Luther, or the other great lords of the Renaissance, and you will have much assurance added to your spirit. Only one thing will be lacking, your freedom as a Christian man.

And of course, you will as a result have nothing to say to those who stand outside this realm of pseudo-submission, of arrogance masquerading as obedience, or to those who are in fact pioneering in all the realms of human enterprise today. For the pre-requisite of being able to speak to others is that you should be with them where they are; not merely exercising your benevolence on their need or your intelligence on their problems; but being truly with them. This being with others and for others, which is the substance of love, is not an individualist manœuvre, but points rather to the grand strategy of real historical life. If your Christian attitude is restricted to the assertion of the self-contained truth of the Word of God understood from within your own situation, then it lacks this essential outgoing movement, the action of love which is poured out, not as pathetic spectacle but as a real encounter of being with being. This lack, which is really a pervasive lovelessness, is apparent in the whole fundamentalist apprehension of the Word of God and the intention of Christianity. The world is denied by such an apprehension. It is set at a distance, and the space between the avowed fundamentalist Christian and the world is not filled, as it can be, and must be, by the action of understanding love. Those 'over there', or 'outside', in the world, are also looking for the gifts which Christianity has to lavish upon them. But they will not find these gifts except in the depths of a personal encounter which includes a being-with them in the whole of their lives and interests.

But the solution is not to be found, either, in the liberalism which is the conventional opponent of fundamentalism. This movement of thought can be ill-defined, for it has ramifications far beyond the matter of how to interpret and understand the Bible. Within the narrower theme, however, liberalism may be described as the effort to extract from the teachings of the Bible certain permanent and timeless truths which may be suitably applied to every human situation. Such truths have been taken to be, for instance, the fatherhood of God, the brotherhood of man, love of your neighbour, belief in the inevitable progress of mankind, and the like. Noble thoughts, indeed; and it would be a shoddy mind which simply laughed at the hopes and ideals of our fathers and grandfathers as these found practical expression in their actions, in politics, in economics, in the great humanitarian and missionary enterprises of last century and the first half of this century. But in the end these ideals have been found inadequate, and the practical good works which flowed directly from them have either come to an end or been assimilated to the residual activities of western civilization. The ideals were inadequate because they were abstractions from the real situation of men. They avoided the historicity of the Christian foundation; so they were not able to face and conquer the evil, or the *Angst*, or the despair, which rises up again and again in the midst of the most ideal situation. The strength of liberalism lies in its recognition of the need for Christianity to be applied to the human situation; its weakness lies in its readiness to discard or to ignore the brute historical scandal of Christianity in order the more readily to apply its tenets to society. For liberal idealism and modernism lose touch with the completeness of the Word of God. They have lost the understanding of it as a historical entity, or rather as a historical situation or event, which rises to its climax in the Incarnate Word but has also manifestations through the whole history of Israel both before and after Christ. In this regard liberalism may be justly accused of making a false and unnecessary concession to a passing phase of humanism, to that sterile and limited anthropology which sees man as completed not in history but in ideas, which sees the Word and the Spirit and God not as historical and encounterable Being but as ideas, and which presupposes and sanctions a spiritualized conception of man which has lost the historical heart of Christianity. The cross, the resurrection and the second coming become, on this view, a shadowy backcloth to an undialectic version of Christianity. The historical tragedy and the consequent seriousness and living nature of the historical triumph of God's work are submerged by an onflowing idea—whether the idea of progress, or of the common goal of all mankind in a grand amalgam of all good ideas and all goodwill which is nicknamed the kingdom of God, or the like—the interruptions to which, from sin, or evil, or death, are seen as no more than casual interruptions. This denial of the actual living historical situation in which man has to live and suffer is really a denial of the reality of man's being as a historical creature, and it bears, incidentally, an ominous resemblance to the Marxist philosophy of the relation of the individual to the

85

idea—which springs of course, from the same idealist seed-bed. In a word, liberalism ends by losing both itself and the Christianity it seeks to serve.

All these proposed remedies—archaism, heteronomism, fundamentalism, liberalism—come to grief because they are based on a partial or distorted understanding of what has been happening to man during the centuries of the modern world. They have their partial and temporary successes because men are often happy to find relief from their pain by any means that lies to hand. When the pain goes as deep as it does today, it is not surprising that a loud voice, or the panoply of authority, can provide the illusion of a real conversion, a turning in the right direction. The shores of the Christian world are littered with the hulks or the jetsam of false loyalties, which have led only to rack and ruin. These illusory invitations are not the only ones to attract people today. A political party, a mass movement, even music, may provide the temporary illusion of an entry into an absolute world. But they are all alike illusory, because they ignore the one inescapable human element, that which makes a man truly human—his personal responsibility—and with bland cruelty they expose what is left of a man, after such a conversion, as another 'head', another number, a swelling of their statistics, a new recruit for their battle against—one another. Or the result may be the very opposite of the false comfort of immersion in a marching herd: it can happen that a man who has sought his assurance, and the truth of his life, in one such grouping will fail to find it and will be left more alone than ever.

It is important to look at this situation of man today with unclouded eyes. Perhaps Martin Buber has made the clearest and most disturbing diagnosis of our state, particularly in his early work *I and Thou*, first published in German as long ago as 1923,[1] and in the later sequel to it published in English in 1947 with the title *Between Man and Man*.[2] In these works he elaborates the two-fold nature of all human life in what he calls an I-It and an I-Thou relation. It is the I-It relation which is dominant in every sphere today; not only in those spheres where it is properly and legitimately active, in experience of using and enjoying, of handling and examining, but also in the spheres where the I-Thou relation should really hold sway, above all in the relations between men. As a result of the failure of the I-Thou relation there has been a loss of the personal, the truly human, throughout the whole world of human activities, and what is left is the alternative, collectivism or individualism. Massification, or isolation: that is the common choice which lies before most people today. Either you walk in step with the rest, doing the things they do, thinking and feeling as they do, and so lose your personal responsibility. Or you rebel, and break free, and enter into isolation. Here too your responsibility withers, for you can be responsible only along with others. Community is the being together of persons in responsible action. But neither collectivism nor individualism permits this kind of responsibility. Collective man is the man without a face, with only a number. He is not a separate responsible person, making his own choices and decisions, he does not meet others in the strength of his own will, and out of the depth of his own being. He has in fact no being of his own, but only illusory being, the chimera of being which he borrows like a cloak from his fellows in the collective. His sign in fact is that cloak or uniform of the collective, and

[1]English translation by R. Gregor Smith, T. & T. Clark, Edinburgh, and Scribner's, New York 1937 (2nd revised ed. 1958).
[2]English translation by R. Gregor Smith, Kegan Paul, Trench, Trübner & Co., London 1947 and Macmillan Co., New York. Also Beacon Press, Boston 1955, and Collins Fontana Library, 1961.

uniformity is the fulfilment at which he aims. Sometimes such a man responds to the despair within himself, or to a call from outside himself, and seeks to escape from the marching herd; he seeks for himself a name and a face. But if he is not ready to enter without reserve into that relation of responsibility which in its highest reaches is characterized by the grave words, 'to love another', then all he is able to find outside himself is—himself. In other words, he is sunk into a more profound isolation than ever, the isolation of the poetic Narcissus, admiring his own image in a pool of water, or the isolation of the philosophic solipsist, finding existence only in himself. He has escaped from the prison of the collective into the romantic tower of his own self.

If these are terrible and searching thoughts when applied to the generality of men today, they become even more terrible when applied to the would-be community of Christians. The consequences are more terrible where the claims are so high. In the sphere of the state, of politics or economics, where a collective or an individual becomes too powerful, or evil, or runs amok, he can still be restrained by war or some other exercise of force, bound and fettered, and put away. But what can you do with a Church that has lost the life of community? It is bad enough if such an organization depends on one of those theological or ritual tendencies, which I have already described, as the explanation and justification of its existence. But it is infinitely worse if such an organization imagines that it thereby possesses community, being-together, *koinonia*. Here you expect to see the fulfilment of human possibilities: people who have come to themselves in the only true way—living, that is, no longer for themselves but for others, within the objective structure of grace. I do not say they live as saints; nor should one distort the issue by demanding that they be born again in the strict evangelical connotation of recent generations. But they must live in openness and expectation of the possibility of being, in an emerging new community. That is, they must live as persons, and not as faceless numbers or as solipsists recognizing no other existence; they must live with and for one another in the extremity of responsible care which is called love.

Has the Church any awareness of its plight? Is there any point where it is trying to communicate, even within its own body, to the breaking-off and dying members? I do not think that the true note of evangelism is being sounded, or that the invitation to life in community is being offered, at any of the points I have described. Nor is it being truly offered in the mass movements of so-called revival which are a marked feature of church life in many places today. The work of the Oxford Groups, or Moral Re-Armament, and the work of Dr Billy Graham, are two examples of this kind of effort. Graham's work is hopelessly constricted to a would-be biblical view of life, which combines a kind of naïve biblicism with an evangelical pietism of the nineteenth century brand, and cannot even envisage the problems of modern man in the death-grip of his false communities. And Moral Re-Armament, which has a longer and more varied record of successes to its credit, is unable to penetrate to the heart of man's position and need today—for so many different reasons that I hardly think it worthwhile attempting to list them. At bottom, Moral Re-Armament, though vividly aware of the deficiencies of the conventional church forms, is itself unable to offer more than a kind of personalist apprehension of certain conventional formulas of old-fashioned evangelism; for here too the biblical apprehension lacks flexibility and depth and range sufficient to turn the history of men in a new direction. Conversion of the classic kind—such as you see at work in men like Moses, and Jeremiah, and Paul, and Augustine—has always meant a new direction for history, conquest of whole new areas for the structure of grace, and a quickened apprehension of the total claim made by the sovereign Lord of history on the historical life of men in society. Such fashionable and even successful movements cannot give us our answer. For they do not disclose an absolute relation to history, they do not lift a man out of the collective or out of his individualism into that free spontaneous and creative life where he can live in the Spirit. They fix men, they do not free them. They bind them to loyalty to a cause, or to a catchword; they smother them in emotions, or swaddle them in old forms. Movements of that kind should be measured not by their success in collecting scalps —I have never heard that the Church should be a kind of scalp-hunter—but by their relation to the total historical possibilities of Christianity in meeting other people, in the place where they are, in all their ambiguity, with an absolute demand for whole-ness and love.

One of the points where I do see hope, where that absolute demand begins to be heard, lies in the work of Rudolf Bultmann. This New Testament scholar has spent the whole of his life in the examination and interpretation of the New Testament writings. In the course of his work he has set many a cat among many pigeons. He was one of the founders of the form-critical method of analyzing and dissecting the Gospels in an effort to recover the genuine sayings lying a generation behind the written tradition of the Church, which is what we possess in our written Gospels. With his writings on demythologizing the New Testament he started a discussion which has been of the utmost benefit for the understanding of faith. This did not pre-vent his own Church from seriously considering whether he should not be arraigned for heresy. His concern has been quite simple: it is to find a way of interpreting and stating the gospel that is apprehensible to modern people. His presupposition, of course, is immense: it is that in fact the gospel is incomprehen-sible to typical modern people. He would, I think, subscribe to the analysis, at least in its broad outlines, which I have been giving you of the predicament in which we have found our-selves since the Renaissance. I mean that he would acknowledge as his presupposition (as it is mine) that a new way of looking at man, and a new conception of man's place in history and responsibility for history, arose with the overthrow of mediaeval civilization. Man ceased to be bound to a specific metaphysic, and was made ready for a new inner-worldly freedom and responsibility which have led him away from the mythological and apocalyptic world view presupposed in the New Testament. In other words, Bultmann sees a new man in being, or in process of being, in becoming, a man with still nothing more than inchoate form, with only the faint outlines of a face and a form —like those great unfinished figures of Michelangelo struggling out of the hard stone from which he intended to shape them. Bultmann is in fact concerned with the clear and conscious emergence of a new possibility in man. In this respect his work demands, what it has not yet received, to be studied in conjunction with the breakdown of old forms in art and letters, in music and writing and painting. The connexion is not a mere coincidence, but indicates a general sense, among the seers and makers, of the new world which is possibly just over the horizon, just round the corner. You may recall how Archbishop Söderblom once defined the Christian apprehension of the kingdom of God as being 'always just round the corner'. It is in this kind of existentialist sense that the vivid potentialities of man can regain their eschatological potency. For Bultmann, though he is ruthless with the primitive Jewish apocalyptic which controls a great deal of the mode of expression of the New Testament, is by no means a liberal who wants to get rid of eschatology. On the contrary, he wishes to restore to Christian life an existentialist eschatology as a force striking out of our future into our present.

A great cry has been raised against his views, echoing from every quarter. There are those who call him an old-fashioned liberal in theology, who merely wants to extract and accommodate the essence of the gospel to passing fashions. There are

91

those who say that by wanting to free the gospel message from its mythological and apocalyptic forms he is attempting the impossible, for the truths of religion must always be clothed in symbols and myths. There are those who say that at all times the gospel has been a scandal to natural man, and Bultmann is simply trying to remove the scandal. I would rather say that in Bultmann we find the effort to restate a doctrine of man which will bear equally upon the churched and the unchurched, on the rump of the Christian world and upon its needy successors, the humanists. He is calling for a radical re-interpretation of the whole body of traditional Christian theology. One thing he is clearly not doing, and that is abandoning the scandal of the historicity and particularity of the Incarnation. Though he finds much in the Gospels which is meaningless and pointless in its present form, since it depends on primitive Jewish apocalyptic or on first-century gnosticism, he does not thereby throw overboard the substance of the *kerygma*. He still asks, with extreme urgency, the burning question, 'How do I become a Christian?' It is the history, and the historicity, which he wants to recover, not as the quintessence of an idealist philosophy, not as a body of alien dogma to be imposed on modern men, with that kind of positivism which says 'Take it or leave it', and not even as a kind of private experience either of the 'numinous' or of outright dependence. Neither Barthianism nor a 'simple' experiential faith of the Schleiermacher-Otto tradition provides, on Bultmann's view, a sufficient understanding either of the historical being of Christianity or of the individual's own being. Bultmann wants to recover the history as a living relation of his being to the structure of grace. 'Faith', he says somewhere, 'is the answer to the question of the *kerygma* which continually addresses me', and it is this *kerygma* which he wishes to uncover in its own life and legitimacy from the mists and twists which it has suffered through one form or another of metaphysical or idealist imposition. It has of course been objected that Bultmann has only replaced one philosophy by another, and that the existentialist philosophy. For it is with the aid of existentialist analysis, in particular that of Heidegger, that he presents his view of man in his natural state. But this analysis, as he himself clearly says, is a descriptive or phenomenological analysis which merely brings us to the threshold: it brings us towards the *kerygma* without pretensions. It is in that situation that it first becomes possible for men really to face the question in the *kerygma* of the historical existence of Jesus.

So far as there is one problem in what I have been saying, we have touched upon it here. It is the problem of the relation of faith to history. When I am invited to believe the gospel, a whole host of problems arises; but chief is this strange question about how it is possible to be related in faith to events which are sunk in the past. This is not merely a question of memory or of certain fixed data, such as knowing that Caesar was murdered, or that William the Conqueror won the battle of Hastings. Both these important events are important because they have a certain effect on our lives, even today, shaping their form and even their content in certain respects whether we know about these events or not. But the relation with the historical events of the life of Jesus is different, for here I am asked to believe that my eternal happiness is at stake. Many answers have been attempted to this question, and to look at them would take us far into the history of religions as well as into the history of Christian dogma. But the guiding clue through the labyrinth seems to me to lie for our day in the hands of Bultmann, when he disentangles from the events an element of transcendence which is not the transcendence of merely wonderful happenings, not the transcendence of a primitive mythology of heaven and earth, not the transcendence expressed in gnosticism (which is no more than an extension of the world, without the conception of a Creator), and not the transcendence expressed in primitive eschatology. But the transcendence which he perceives in the

93

Christ-event is a transcendence which shines through history, where grace springs up as it were in the midst of human life, where responsibility is absolute, where the individual is invited to decide towards an objective possibility of grace. This is the kind of conversion which lifts the subject out of himself, out of his fears and his sins, into a forgiven life. Thenceforth he is open to the world and to others, he is at peace. He is no longer confident in himself, boasting in the flesh; but his confidence is in the eternal Thou who is present through the given Word, recurrent in each personal situation of responsibility. This is the meeting of man with God which takes place, in faithful response, in human history. This is neither a metaphysical assertion about God's attributes, nor an emotional excitation in face of the unknowable Eternal. 'To know Christ is to know his benefits', said the young Melanchthon; and 'we cannot know God as he is, but only in what he does to us', said Wilhelm Herrmann, Bultmann's own teacher in Marburg. In the day-to-day decisions of the responsible person, in every sphere with which he has to do, this absolute meeting may be disclosed. It is not an extra to those day-to-day events, but appears in and through them. It is truer to say that God is met through the world than over and above it. He comes not 'plumb down from above', but is to be glimpsed in every event, in every needy hand upraised, every conflict of will, every utterance of hope or love. This relation of faith to history, then, is made possible by the initiating action of God's grace throughout history; in the incarnate Word supremely, but not there alone. This Word comes to us out of history because it comes to us now, in our present. Past history is real, and related to us, because it is not past, but present.

Further, this presence of past history, this true historism is filled out and confirmed not by the past alone, but by the potentialities contained in the past, i.e., by the future. The potentialities of the Word are boundless, but they are not vague.

They are explicitly and clearly contained within human history. That is to say, past and future combine in the present. The Incarnate Word is focused ever anew in the present history of man. The future is as important as the past. The mythology of the second coming is intended to tell us something not about some ineffable cosmic conclusion, some supra-historical and therefore unhistorical end to history, but about the fullness of history itself. What began as history, and has meaning as present history, cannot end as anything but history without emptying the reality out of the whole of history, and therefore, of course, out of the historical Incarnation as the concentrated climax of God's speech with men. Again and again we find that the drift, the temptation, the easy way out, for Christian faith is towards the denial of the historicity of faith as the supreme moment towards which God is inviting his world. But the Lord of history who will come again will not destroy history, nor will he cap it with something incomprehensible to and different from history. The faith in him who will come again is an indissoluble part of the historicity of God's purpose. Man is not meant to be cast down by the awful premonition of the trumpet of the Lord sounding in his ears. Rather he is intended to hear it as a clarion call rising out of the triumph of God within history. This triumph has already been achieved. Only its celebration awaits us. In this sense the second coming is not different from the first coming. To continue the mythological idiom, the trumpet is sounding to the ears of faith in every present situation, putting a period to history, indeed, but thereby making and not destroying that history. So we may legitimately speak of the future being contained in the past, the second coming in the first coming, and all history lying open before us. It is in this confidence that the Christian can see man rising to new heights over and beyond the dark valleys of sin and despair and death, by which he believes himself today (as every man in his own day) to be specially tempted. Confidence is available to the man who lives by faith

95

so far as he lives in and through the forgiveness offered to him by God's dealing with all history, past, present and future, and so far as he lives, in consequence, with an open mind, free for his responsibilities, open and free towards all that may come. This is the eschatology which releases us from bondage to a mythology, and proleptically brings before us, in our present commitments, all the glory and certainty of the end. It is a historical end, that is all we can say about it. We cannot predict its form, we cannot imagine its nature. History is full of surprises, for it is the conspiracy, rather, the public covenant, between God and man; and neither man nor God is fettered. In the freedom of the invitation and the freedom of the response history moves freely towards its unimagined goal.

It is in the setting of this kind of faith that we have to consider still the positive possibilities open to us in our present history, and these I hope to suggest in my next chapter.

VI

This-Worldly Transcendence

In this chapter I want to indicate what seems to me to be the way through the impasse for proper belief—a way which leads ultimately, of course, to practical demands and consequences for Christian action. Here, however, I am concerned only with the presuppositions of a new theology of man, an anthropotheology, which may be adequate to what I believe to be the immense future still awaiting our society if it can come to a proper understanding of itself.

So far I have been talking of failures: the failure of the Renaissance, and the failure of the Reformation. The Renaissance failed to follow out the logic of its own maturity by means of a full doctrine of man; and the Reformation failed to apprehend the full freedom offered to it by the breaking of the mediaeval metaphysical bonds. There has been a series of attempts to fight for a solution, but in the main the heirs of the Renaissance have worked on without hope, and the heirs of the Reformation have proposed solutions which have been little more than rearguard actions in defence of untenable positions. The gulf between the conventional Christian position and the position of ordinary unchurched men has been traversed by Bultmann, in the effort at demythologizing which I sketched in the previous chapter. But in the main this effort has not been acceptable to the churches. His traversal has been solitary, precarious, and no more accessible to an ordinary man than, say, the first flight across the Channel by Blériot was repeatable by any Tom, Dick or Harry. With time and labour this pioneer effort will work its way into the tradition, but not yet, and not easily. Meantime, the characteristic position of ordinary men is either that they are bundled together in some kind of collective, or that they are isolated in a kind of individualism which offers no hope of community. In either case community is hardly known. Even friendship, or love, which are the high points of real community between persons, seem to be increasingly rare.

What of the Christian in all this? What are his real commitments and obligations? Where is his community, the Church, the new creation? And if I ask the most urgent and personal question of all, 'What must I do to be saved?', I intend no blasphemy or ultimate scepticism when I say that the answer given to the jailer's question in the Book of Acts, 'Believe on the Lord Jesus Christ' does not answer my question, today, in my circumstances—the historical circumstances I have described—directly or satisfactorily. It leaves me, and my companions in this modern world, both those within and those outside the Church, with many questions, the question about the nature of belief, the question about who Jesus is, and where, and how, and the question about the substance of salvation itself. In other words, a great deal of re-thinking requires to be done which will be neither biblical theology by itself nor systematic theology by itself, but an existential assessment of the Bible and the world which will uncover the almost entirely dissipated claim of real transcendence as an existent force *within* this world.

One of the most illuminating entries into this whole complex of questions has been made by Dietrich Bonhoeffer. In his *Letters and Papers from Prison*[1] you see a fine, cultured, sensitive mind, heir of all the wealth of Europe, rejoicing in its treasures, but at the same time intensely concerned with the problem of the right way through for modern man to his proper life as the heir of Christianity. How to become a Christian was Bonhoeffer's

[1] S.C.M. Press, London 1967 (3rd revised and enlarged edition). As *Prisoner for God*, Macmillan Co., New York 1959.

problem, as it was Kierkegaard's. There is one little section in this volume of fragments and teasing hints which bears the simple title 'Outline for a Book'. Bonhoeffer says in three pages more than most men might say in three hundred pages. He sketches the plan for a book of three chapters. The first chapter was to deal with the coming of age of humanity, the parallel decay of religion, and the failure, in the last analysis, of the Protestant churches, and even of the great battling Confessing Church during the Nazi régime in Germany. The second chapter was to draw out the real meaning of the Christian faith in terms of the significant heading 'Worldliness and God': what we mean by God, and the consequent re-interpretation of biblical terminology, of the cultus, and the creeds. The last chapter was to draw out the consequences for the actual existing Church. I quote now from that short last chapter:

> The Church is the Church only when it exists for others. To make a start, it should give away all its property to those in need. The clergy must live solely on the free-will offerings of their congregations, or possibly engage in some secular calling. The Church must share in the secular problems of ordinary human life, not dominating, but helping and serving.[1]

I do not think that Bonhoeffer is merely repeating here familiar exhortations to piety and good works. He is certainly not indifferent to the power of concrete example, drawing this as he does direct from its source in the humanity of Jesus. But the clue to his revolutionary thought is to be found in his fresh understanding of two things, the world and God. He does not think of these as separate entities of such a kind that you might possess and use your separate apprehension of God for a suitable assault upon the world. He says explicitly, in this same 'Outline for a Book', that the experience of transcendence is to

---

[1] *op. cit.* p211.

be found in 'the concern of Jesus for others'. In other words, the transcendent is met in the solicitude for others as given to us in the life and way of Jesus. This has also an important negative implication, namely, that God is not to be met primarily in some assertion about him. God is not to be found in an abstract belief about his omnipotence, or omniscience, or even in the idea of love. God is not the idea we have of him. He is not any idea. To attempt to elevate some idea to the place of God is to make an idol and worship that instead of God. When we set up some abstraction in place of God we are worshipping nothing more than an extension of the world. This kind of false worship has led to all kinds of perversions in the history of the Church, which has always been too ready to act on behalf of God, assuming a familiarity with God which has led it to the ultimate blasphemy of killing men in the name of God and his love.

This is a moral failure. But this confusion between God and our dogmatic assertions about him has led to an intellectual as well as a moral failure. We have been all too ready, especially since the great breakthrough of the Renaissance, to fight a kind of battle against the world on behalf of God. Here too the Church has desired, as it were, to rescue God from the consequences of his own recklessness first in creating and then in saving his world. God's liberating action in his Word—which as I have repeatedly said can be seen as truly liberating only when it is seen as more than an isolated occurrence in history— has been disallowed by the common-sense of Christian people as altogether too dashing, too audacious and foolhardy. So when the breakthrough of man's spirit beat back the Christian warrior from one entrenched position after another, the Christian response in recent centuries has varied little. Before the advancing battalions of intelligence and reason and scepticism, as one area of knowledge after another was captured for technology, or science, or psychology, God has been rescued by too willing hands. The children of light have been happily engaged in drawing God back into the darkness, beyond the frontiers of assured life, into the region which is euphemistically called the mystery of God. The mystery of God has been equated with a kind of *terra incognita*, an as-yet unknowable rather than as a truly ineffable mystery, which is to say a *present* mystery whose mystery is an actual, encountered, lived experience of an incomprehensible but not inapprehensible gift. The consequences of this series of retreats have been distortion of the understanding of God, confusion among the ranks on both sides, and dishonour of God's name. For in fact by thus attempting to safeguard God, the Church has only been safeguarding its idea of God. It has been honouring not the incarnate Word in the bleeding helplessness of utter service, but an emasculated Jesus, the Jesus of the *Ersatz* gold halo and the tawdry pietism of decadent Jesusology. It has been honouring not the God in the midst of the world but a kind of escape mechanism devised by its own fears. In one magnificent letter, written while bombing raids were being carried out over his prison, Bonhoeffer sums up the confusion of the Church in our time in these words:

'While I am often reluctant to mention God by name to religious people—because that name somehow seems to me here not to ring true, and I feel myself to be slightly dishonest (it is particularly bad when others start to talk in religious jargon; I then dry up almost completely and feel awkward and uncomfortable)—to people with no religion I can on occasion mention him by name quite calmly and as a matter of course. Religious people speak of God when human knowledge (perhaps simply because they are too lazy to think) has come to an end, or when human resources fail—in fact it is always the *deus ex machina* that they bring on to the scene, either for the apparent solution of insoluble problems, or as strength in human failure—

101

always, that is to say, exploiting human weakness or human boundaries. Of necessity, that can go on only till people can by their own strength push these boundaries somewhat further out, so that God becomes superfluous as a *deus ex machina*. I have come to be doubtful of talking about any human boundaries (is even death, which people now hardly fear, and is sin, which they now hardly understand, still a genuine boundary today?). It always seems to me that we are trying anxiously in this way to reserve some space for God; I should like to speak of God not on the boundaries but at the centre, not in weaknesses but in strength; and therefore not in death and guilt but in man's life and goodness. As to the boundaries, it seems to me better to be silent and leave the insoluble unsolved . . . God is beyond in the midst of our life. The church stands, not at the boundaries where human powers give out, but in the middle of the village.'[1]

This powerful recognition of the place of God in his world springs from Bonhoeffer's understanding of the nature of the encounter with Jesus. 'Faith,' he says, 'is participation in this being of Jesus (incarnation, cross, and resurrection). Our relation to God is not a "religious" relationship to the highest, most powerful, and best Being imaginable—that is not authentic transcendence—but our relation to God is a new life in "existence for others", through participation in the being of Jesus. The transcendental is not infinite and unattainable tasks, but the neighbour who is within reach in any given situation. God in human form—not, as in oriental religions, in animal form, monstrous, chaotic, remote, and terrifying, nor in the conceptual forms of the absolute, metaphysical, infinite, etc., nor yet in the Greek divine-human form of "man in himself",

[1] *op. cit.* p154f.

but "the man for others", and therefore the Crucified, the man who lives out of the transcendent.'[1]

This understanding of the encounter with Jesus proposes a dialectic of transcendence which can, I think, lead us through our modern impasse. On the one hand there is here a recognition of the status of the world as the place to which Jesus came, the place where he was Jesus and, as a consequence of which he is what he is. This leads Bonhoeffer to his repeated but alas not fully elaborated remarks about what he calls worldliness or religionlessness. In one letter he says:

'What is bothering me incessantly is the question what Christianity really is, or indeed who Christ really is, for us today. The time when people could be told everything by means of words, whether theological or pious, is over, and so is the time of inwardness and conscience—and that means the time of religion in general. We are moving towards a completely religionless time; people as they now are simply cannot be religious any more. Even those who honestly describe themselves as "religious" do not in the least act up to it, and so they presumably mean something quite different by "religious". Our whole nineteen-hundred-year-old Christian preaching and theology rest on the "religious a priori" of mankind. "Christianity" has always been a form—perhaps the true form—of "religion". But if one day it becomes clear that this a priori does not exist at all, but was a historically conditioned and transient form of human self-expression, and if therefore man becomes radically religionless—and I think that that is already more or less the case already (else how is it, for example, that this war, in contrast to all previous ones, is not calling forth any "religious" reaction?)—what does that mean for "Christianity"? . . .

How can Christ become the Lord of the religionless as well? Are there religionless Christians? If religion is only a garment of Christianity—and even this garment has looked very different at different times—then what is a religionless Christianity? . . . What do a church, a community, a sermon, a liturgy, a Christian life mean in a religionless world? How do we speak of God—without religion . . .? How do we speak . . . in a "secular" way about "God"? In what way are we "religionless-secular" Christians . . . not regarding ourselves from a religious point of view as specially favoured, but rather as belonging wholly to the world? In that case Christ is no longer an object of religion, but something quite different, really the Lord of the world.'[1]

I am quite sure that in such letters Bonhoeffer was breaking through to a fresh apprehension of the status of man and the world as something existing in their own right as the place where God loves to be. You might say that he was reaching a new apprehension of the meaning of this world, and ourselves, as creation, as creatures; but it was not an abstract or isolated apprehension, but closely connected, indeed flowing out of, his apprehension of Christ as Lord of the world. That, at least, seems to have been the intention of the remarks he has made in such letters, though in fact it is not so easy to see how he could, out of such views, ever have constructed an orthodox doctrine of the relation of Christ to the Father.

The important point for our thoughts, however, is the tension between this affirmation about man and the world, about man's worldliness and religionlessness, and the other side of Bonhoeffer's position. It is this other side which holds Bonhoeffer from degenerating into a stoic position about the world in its self-sufficiency. He calls it *Arkandisziplin*, arcane or secret discipline. This is the heart of his thought, but it would be

[1] *op. cit.* p52-4.

wrong to think of it as a kind of individualist retreat, a kind of cultivation of inwardness or even a search for personal salvation. He rightly points out that in the Old Testament there is really nothing said about saving one's soul, and in the New Testament the focus of everything is righteousness and the kingdom of God. 'It is not,' he writes, 'with the beyond that we are concerned, but with this world as created and preserved, and subjected to laws, reconciled and renewed.'[1] What sustains him is nothing very original, but it is the climax as well as the ground of all his belief. It is a kind of humorous, humble, self-effacing secrecy of devotion and hope, which finds no counterpart in the visible world, nothing in symbol or gesture by which it may be fully reflected and expressed; nothing in the cult or the ritual which may presume to take its place. I do not mean that Bonhoeffer denied or decried the place of symbol and gesture and ritual; only they were secondary, part of that special development of responses and expressions of faith which are summed up as 'religion'. Bonhoeffer was looking past these things to the form for his faith which actually could meet the world, actually be in it, without reserve, as Christ was in it. He would have quoted with approval the saying of Tillich that Jesus came in order to destroy religion. That faith itself rested on the sketchy and strange tradition within Christianity of secrecy, exclusiveness, fastidiousness, which has never received great prominence. It is the tradition whose origins lie in the same region as the origins of the doctrine of election; but it has a different bent and outcome. 'Cast not your pearls before swine'; 'shake off the dust of that city from your feet'; 'this is my body': these are all sayings which presuppose, indeed demand, a kind of initiation and secrecy which clearly forbids the intrusion of the curious or the self-certain. The words of Christ are for all, indeed, and the powerful strain of universalism has

[1] *op. cit.* p156 (translation slightly altered).

swept Christianity along many triumphant lines. Paul's equally powerful stress on the givenness, the gift, of God's grace, combines with this universalism to keep the idea of secrecy and exclusiveness from too great prominence in Christian history. Nevertheless it is there, and the simplicities of the gospel, the call to be humble, and unostentatious in prayer, never using naked power, but always service, and sacrifice, are both its sustenance and its preservative.

The real strength and significance of this secret discipline, however, is its persistent pushing of the believer back into the world. He may not escape, as Reinhold Niebuhr once remarked that theological students tend to do, when they are faced with an insoluble problem: by quitting grappling, and taking an elevator to the eternal. The Christian discipline does not permit such an escape, for it is not really interested in such a conception of the eternal at all.

These two elements, then, the worldliness of God and the secret discipline, come together in a powerful dialectic in Bonhoeffer's thought. The Christian will remain in the tension of this dialectic all his days. Any interpretation of the Christian dialectic in other terms, such as the tension of the kingdom that is realized and the kingdom that is still to come, or the tension of this world and the next, of earth and heaven, rests upon a too narrow conception of eschatology or a too naïve acceptance of the old mythology. The real dialectic, as Bonhoeffer has sketched it, does not find God in the cult, taken by itself; nor in any form of pietism or socialism, which are just two forms of escape from one side or the other of the dialectic. But this dialectic of commitment to the world demands complete responsibility in and for the world, in all its interests and problems.

Of course there are perils here, on the one hand the peril of irresponsible acquiescence in the way of the world as a self-sufficient entity, and on the other hand the peril of complete invisibility, of the practical non-existence of the secret discipline.

It is hard for faith to stand the strain of a profession whose perfection consists in its not professing itself, or rather, which confirms its reality not by assertion but by submission, not by taking over the world, but by identifying itself with the world, not by resting content with just crying 'Lord, Lord', but by living in and for the same world which has now been reconciled. But this is the necessary dialectic. You are both for the world, with all the strength of the given situation, and against it; against it not as an intellectual rationalization of inaction and absolute denial of the world, but against it in the depth of this existential dialectic. The Christian cannot be indifferent to this world which God made and loves. Yet how can he be other than against it in its evil and sin and hopelessness? Both positions are necessary, and both at the same time, and without reserve. This is the depth and inwardness of the affliction with which Christ was afflicted; more, it is the filling up of what is lacking in that affliction with the whole joyous agony of the historical failure and the historical possibilities of man.

The question which arises most acutely within this dialectic is whether there is any room left for positive evangelism. Does the evangelist not bring a message with authority? Does he not proclaim, like a herald, the message of his Lord? This is so. But the form we are bound to give the question is just this: whether the real evangelism in our day is not rather that kind of identification with the world in its griefs and joys and achievements and self-questionings—in other words, in the maturity of the world in its self-understanding, as Bonhoeffer puts it—than the imposition of a foreign body of traditional concepts upon that world. To help the world to come to itself, rather than to attempt to shake it out of itself—is that not what has happened at the great turning-points of history? St Augustine's theology for instance, which shaped a thousand years of Christian history, sprang from the very situation in which he was placed, with Rome fallen and the barbarians at the gates. He could not save

107

his diocese, or his land; but out of his work the new Christendom of the West arose.

In our situation today we cannot command the same solutions. In particular, we cannot simply bring in the mythological or the metaphysical views of transcendence with their basic premise of the religiousness of man. This does not mean that we have to abandon a doctrine of the Word of God; but it does mean that we seek another way of expressing our encounter with the majesty of the sovereign Lord of history. For the old doctrine, based on a metaphysics of distinction between the place of God and the place of man, has sunk until the effort to assert the majestic otherness of God has become merely an ineffective way of asserting man's own imprisonment within the world. The old doctrine of transcendence is nothing more than an assertion of an outmoded view of the world. The enormity of God's action in giving himself to the world in the Incarnation is no longer properly apprehended in the old way of thinking. The doctrine of the Word degenerates into pietist Jesusology or into a frantic greed to possess and manage the Word. Either way the world is not taken in full seriousness. But in the Incarnation God has affirmed the world, and affirmed history, and the particularity of history, in such a way that it is simply impossible to confine our apprehension of him to a metaphysical elaboration of the event of the Incarnation. The power of that event can be properly faced only in the logic of that event itself. Some way of meeting that event without reserve and without reduction has to be found. We call the way of meeting and accepting it *faith*. But again, this is not a relation to some otherwise inconceivable transcendence; it is not the so-called mystical apprehension of the unknowable. But this relation of faith finds its room within the sphere of historical human activity and nowhere else. And I mean by that sphere the *whole* sphere of human activity, in which the religious element is only a part, and if my diagnosis is right a diminishing part. I should

say, to take an extreme and provocative example, that we must
be ready to take quite seriously even the implications of an
avowed atheist like Feuerbach in his momentous wrestling with
the problem of God's being and human existence. I quote a few
sentences from his early work on *The Essence of Christianity*: Feuerbach in this passage was particularly concerned to disprove the
need for believing in God as a special existence, with special
proofs for his existence provided in the form of miracles and
other special effects, and to that extent, of course, he was en-
gaging in the old discussion of the *Aufklärung* for and against
special revelation. But in the drift of his thought I believe he was
not far off from that fresh understanding of transcendence
which I have been bringing to your attention. He writes:

> 'The belief in the existence of God is the belief in a special
> existence, separate from the existence of man and of nature.
> A special existence can only be proved in a special manner.
> This faith is therefore only a true and living one when
> special effects, immediate appearances of God, miracles,
> are believed in. Where, on the other hand, the belief in
> God is identified with belief in the world, where the belief
> in God is no longer a special faith, where the general being
> of the world takes possession of the whole man, there
> vanishes also the belief in special effects and appearances of
> God. Belief in God is wrecked, stranded on the belief in the
> world, in natural effects as the only true ones. As here the
> belief in miracles is no longer anything more than the
> belief in historical, past miracles, so the existence of God is
> also only an historical, in itself atheistic conception.'[1]

If you have followed me so far, then you will see that the interesting thing about this argument of Feuerbach's is that he is

[1]Ludwig A. Feuerbach *The Essence of Christianity* English translation by George
Eliot of the 2nd edition of 1843, Trübner & Co., London 1881, p203. Also
available in Harper Torchbooks, New York 1957.

pleading against the old arguments about the transcendent power of God for what he calls a historical existence of God. That he identifies this 'historical' with 'atheistic' is, I think, an unnecessary deviation from his own argument. A faith which takes us not out of this world, into a sphere of arbitrary interventions, but deeper into the world in its historicity, is, it seems to me, the very crux of our belief in the historical Incarnation. In this historical Word of God we see nothing arbitrary, but the endless pressure of God through the events, the things and the people and the situations, of his world. We cannot be in a closer relation to God than the one he himself provides by means of his own modest pressure upon us. I can quote Luther here, as Feuerbach also does in that same argument, who said:

> 'We have as yet so to do with God as with one hidden from us, and it is not possible that in this life we should hold communion with him face to face. All creatures are now nothing else than vain masks, under which God conceals himself, and by which he deals with us.'[1]

'As yet,' says Luther, and 'vain masks'; thereby he shows the longing of the Christian for the ultimate meeting, face to face, for the blessed vision. But it is possible to hold this belief as an originating power for our faith, without our needing to enquire further into it, far less to raise a new structure of ideas to try and explain the life beyond death. Here in this life, as Luther with all his transcendental reservations clearly sees, God deals with us by and through the other creatures. This is the way in which an understanding of transcendence can come alive in our faith: within the manifold forms of God's creation and creativity his Word recurs, in our present being. God is met in his works and gifts, not in himself, and not in an idea of him. He is met at the luminous point of human existence, where the individual faces him in utter openness, receives forgiveness, and is made free.

[1] *ibid.* p190.

But this facing of God is always in and through, and not other than or additional to, the facing of other people in the emergent community with them. The eternal is in time, heaven is through earth, the supernatural not other than the natural, the spiritual not more than the wholly human: all these categories dissolve in the power of the one real relation, the two-fold relation to people and things. Here is the real place where man is made new. The new man is man in community with man in the strength of the given grace which meets him as tasks and responsibilities and opening freedoms in actual situations in their wholeness.

This is the real hope for the world. The hope for the Church, the hope for Christendom are secondary matters. We may hope that out of the living encounter with God, within the structure of grace, of the given situation, the tenuous, fragmentary web which holds together in the delicate bonds of responsible freedom all those who are turned out from themselves, into the needs and enterprises of the world—we may hope that out of this encounter new history may be made.

It is out of such turning, such returns into the freedom offered to us, that history has always been made. It is unpredictable, surprising, having effects beyond calculation or expectation. For this encounter is the burning point, the crux, the one truly live point in the whole story of mankind: the point where a man, in the full depth of his humanity, with the whole burden of his memories which we call culture and the whole burden of his failures and sin, takes to himself, in his whole life, the words of forgiveness and the invitation to faith which are the palimpsest of all the pages of history.

VII

The Crisis about God

There is a crisis about God today. I make this statement deliberately as general and as widely cast as possible. It implies a whole range of crises, and is therefore by no means a simple statement. All that I wish to do here is to indicate some of the points at which we may recognize a crisis. I want then to suggest how I think the crisis may be overcome.

The first, and for the theologians the most obvious, form in which the crisis is apparent is to be found in the fashionable question whether it is possible at all to speak about God. What I said in my last chapter, in deploying some of Bonhoeffer's thoughts, about the difficulty of constructing today an orthodox doctrine of the relation of Christ to the Father, is amply illustrated by many of those who have learned from Bonhoeffer. One of the most distinguished of them is Paul van Buren. His reliance upon Jesus, the man for others, the man with the infectious freedom, follows in a clear line from one side of Bonhoeffer's thought. But he answers the question, whether God-language is possible at all, with a clear No; and this is an equally clear departure from the ambivalence of Bonhoeffer's thought. Bonhoeffer could never have said, as van Buren says: 'whatever men were looking for in looking for "God" is to be found by finding Jesus of Nazareth.'[1]

Van Buren's problem is set—one might even say dictated—for him by his submission to a somewhat passing demand, made

[1]Paul van Buren *The Secular Meaning of the Gospel* S.C.M. Press, London and Macmillan Co., New York 1963, p147.

by the analytic philosophers in their first enthusiasm, that meaningful statements must be empirically verifiable. In recent years analytic philosophy is much more sophisticated, and is ready to take account of various 'language games', or, as we might more simply say, various contexts of experience.

But even in a wider context than that offered by the demand for verification, the question still arises, 'How can I talk of God?' What sense does it make to talk of God? Rudolf Bultmann asked the question explicitly as long ago as 1925, in an essay entitled, 'Welchen Sinn hat es, von Gott zu reden?' What meaning does it have to talk of God? In brief, his argument is that you cannot talk *about* God, for that would mean regarding God as an object in the world who is at your disposal. You can only talk of God in the recognition of faith that you are a sinner, but a forgiven sinner, and this makes a whole world of difference. It makes, in fact, your world different. 'Faith is the archimedean point, which shakes the world to its foundations and makes it God's world.'[1]

Quite early in his career, therefore, Bultmann both perceived, and set about clarifying, the meaning of the modern crisis in the whole way of doing theology, of understanding what its method is, what its limits are, and what its possibilities as a viable discipline for today are. This has often centred on the dispute whether it can be called a science or not—as in the famous series of public letters exchanged between Adolf von Harnack and the young Karl Barth.[2]

In order to indicate where on my view the crisis leads us, and how it may be overcome, I shall have to return to the strictly

[1]Rudolf Bultmann *Glauben und Verstehen* J. C. B. Mohr (Paul Siebeck), Tübingen 1961 Vol I p37: this particular essay is printed in English in The Christian Scholar *XLIII*, 3, (1960) pp213-22 and the quotation above occurs on p221.
[2]The correspondence is reprinted in Karl Barth *Theologische Fragen und Antworten* Evangelischer Verlag, Zollikon 1957, pp7-31.

theological problem. But the strictly theological problem is both a reflection of, and an active influence upon, the underlying situation of faith. It is, once again, a question of man, of man's identity, of man's self-understanding, which faces us here. Even for the theologian, therefore, the question about God turns into a question about man. And the theology which can tackle this two-fold question must be an anthropological theology, or an anthropotheology. The crisis about God is also a crisis of faith. The two go together, and there is an interaction of the one upon the other. Theology is reflection upon faith, and if the one is in crisis, so must the other be.

How may we define this side of the crisis, the crisis of faith? It is easy for the teacher of religion to point to various experiences: the increasing loss of any link with the tradition of theological thinking, of worship and ritual, the sheer ignorance of the material of the traditions which have made our society; and again, the overwhelming concern with material and empirical interests, joined with a pathetic trust in the possibilities of technological manipulation of life and of the world's resources to produce a reasonable and perhaps even a happy *modus vivendi*. The children in our schools merely reflect in all this the styles of the whole of society. I should sum up this side of the crisis as a loss of the sense of transcendence—at least in the generally accepted understanding of transcendence, namely, an other-worldly sphere which impinges upon this world in the extraordinary demands of religion. If religion in this context survives at all, then it does so as an individual taste, or whim, and as operating within a limited area of the individual's interests. It becomes essentially an individual and private matter. The form may vary: it may be pietist, or quietist, or both together: in any case it is regarded by the generality as an optional extra to the business of living.

But, it might be said, neither the theological crisis nor the more general crisis of faith necessarily means that there is a crisis about God. Strictly speaking, it might be said, we are only observing a modern version of the old story: man is a sinner, he chooses to rebel, and to be separated from God. In Buber's language we could then speak of an *eclipse* of God. 'An eclipse of the sun is something that takes place between the sun and our eyes, not in the sun itself.'[1] The implication in Buber's assessment of the crisis is that God is still there, he is not in a crisis, but man is.

If this were the extent of the crisis, then we might well say that all we need is the courage of our convictions, and the ability to express these convictions in language suited to the time, and with patience and determination we should move to a different position, where we should no longer be in a state of eclipse with God.

It is here that the theologians return to the field, with even more devastating assertions. The so-called 'death-of-God' theologians are in their various ways going beyond Nietzsche who said that God is dead, for Nietzsche (if I understand him aright[2]) was really speaking of the death of an idea of God; but a man like Thomas J. J. Altizer is intending something different. He is speaking of a death of God which was consummated in the self-emptying of God in Christ, who was crucified, dead, and buried. This is clearly the statement of a fairly sophisticated theologian. It is closely connected with a position of faith. That is to say, the faith which is regarded by Altizer as still viable is one which has abandoned all relationship with an 'exalted

[1]Martin Buber *The Eclipse of God* Victor Gollancz, London and Harper & Row, New York 1952 p34. Also available in Harper Torchbooks.
[2]There is an interesting suggestion, in a hitherto unpublished thesis on Nietzsche by one of my students, Ronald Carson (Glasgow 1968), that Nietzsche is speaking rather in an ethical than an idealist strain, and means that men by their actions have murdered God, but at the same time that God allowed himself, out of pity for men, to be slain. If this is correct, then Altizer is theologizing on the basis of the second part of Nietzsche's idea.

Lord', or 'the proclaimer of an already distant and alien majesty of God'.[1] While it is a faith that rejoices in the 'death' of this exalted and transcendent God, positively it finds its assurance in and through the 'historical realization of the death of God' in Christ's death, which is then regarded as making possible 'the full unfolding of the forward movement of the Incarnation'.[2] Altizer has thus succeeded, in his theological analysis, in dealing with the critical loss of transcendence. He has done so by translating transcendence into 'the actuality of life and experience', that is, into our historical world conceived of as entirely immanent. Christ has become a part of the process of history, that, and no more. 'It is precisely because the movement of the Incarnation has now become manifest in every human hand and face, dissolving even the memory of God's original transcendent life and redemptive power, that there can no longer be either a truly contemporary movement to transcendence or an active and living faith in the transcendent God.'[3]

So far, then, we have seen that there is a crisis in God-language, there is a crisis in the kind of faith regarded as appropriate to the modern world, and there is a crisis about God which at its most acute might be regarded as the desire to lose oneself in *nihil*. Altizer, certainly, comes very near to a this-worldly mysticism in which faith loses itself, not in an *O altitudo*, but in the historical process regarded as its own self-contained justification.

If these three forms of the crisis, that of God-language, that of faith, and that of God in himself, were simply separable, then it would be conceivable that one or other of the forms of the crisis might be overcome. But this is not so. They are three

---

[1]*The Gospel of Christian Atheism* Westminster Press, Philadelphia 1966 and Collins, London 1967 p134.
[2]*op. cit.* p135.   [3]*op. cit.* p136.

forms of the one crisis. The presence of the theological crisis means that faith has now no way of formulating itself, it has no unassailable model, and no certain and assured style. Even the Bible as a model is on the run. Faith is therefore not only suffering from the breakdown of forms and the relativizing of models. It has actually lost its reality because it has lost a form. Faith needs language, and if language itself is called in doubt, faith cannot survive. The old metaphysic by which transcendence was expressed is no longer viable; the central doctrine of Christian faith, concerning the connexion between Christ and the Father, has so far found no convincing modern expression. In this débacle God has gone under.

The way forward is only possible by looking back. When an accident has happened, we naturally want to get at the reasons for it. When the accident takes the form of a universal posting of 'missing believed dead' in respect of God, we still—all the more so—want to find out the reasons. This effort I now want to make.

I restrict myself to the theological form of the crisis. Others may find it possible to re-establish the life of faith in terms of practical obedience and service, and I do not decry such a possibility. There is even the chance that disciplined experiment with certain forms of meditation might lead to a blossoming of something like a mystical practice. But of this I personally am by temperament and training more sceptical. Of the value, or rather of the absence of value, in mass revivals, I am pretty certain: that is, so long as they rely upon an outmoded theological scheme they can only confuse the issue.

The real theological issue involves a retracing of our steps, through almost the whole classic tradition of theology. This tradition has, I believe, been bedevilled by a constant temptation to avert attention from the thorough-going historicity of faith This has taken various forms, such as the docetic form, in which man's world has been more or less written off in favour of a

117

'spiritual' realm which can be 'known' by the elect, the *illuminati*. It has also taken the subtler form, right in the midst of orthodoxy, of conceiving of God as a being, an entity, alongside other beings, certainly the supreme being, the entity 'which has most being, the *ens realissimum*,'[1] but all the same a being, who may therefore be located, in heaven, or in eternity, or in a transcendent metaphysically conceived realm; and who may be discussed, examined, provided with attributes, and even, *mirabile dictu*, proven to exist.[2]

The philosophical assumption behind this way of conceiving of God is that man's experience is capable of being analyzed in terms of himself as the conceiving subject, and everything else, including God, as the object of that conceiving.

John Macquarrie, who points this out in the essay on 'The Language of Being', to which I have already referred, is concerned, as he says, 'to restore the oldest tradition of all' (in philosophy), namely, that which is concerned not with beings or entities but with Being, and he thinks that this Being may be interpreted as revealing itself in such a way that the believer 'cannot withhold the response of worship and commitment'.[3]

The immense problems which are opened up by Professor Macquarrie's suggestion—and by a great many other of his recent writings, especially *Principles of Christian Theology*—cannot be more than indicated here. In another place I intend to examine in more detail the whole problem involved in the traditional concept of being—ontological language—in connexion with the doctrine of God.[4] Meantime, I wish just to indicate that I should go another way about replacing the broken-down conception of God as *a* being. Briefly, I should say

---

[1] Cf. John Macquarrie *Studies in Christian Existentialism* S.C.M. Press, London and Westminster Press, Philadelphia 1966 p94.
[2] *op. cit.* p95.   [3] *ibid.*
[4] Cf. my forthcoming Warfield Lectures *The Doctrine of God*.

that we are only involved in speculation, unanchored to historical experience, when we speak of God either as a being or a Being. God and man belong together, and we can only speak of God in speaking of what he does to us, to echo Wilhelm Herrmann's well-known words. It is therefore—at least in our time —only possible to talk of God within the situation of existence, that is, of human existence. This situation may involve a relation or a disrelation to God. The possibility of talking about God is not circumscribed by the self-understanding of faith of a positive kind, but may include the serious question and self-understanding of one who cannot commit himself to what he understands faith to demand of him. In either case the situation carries God within it, as it were, as the possibility of human existence. God can therefore not be spoken of as a being alongside other beings. But neither can he be spoken of simply as Being, or as in 'is-ness'. He can only be spoken of in terms of what he does in our historical existence.

This means that he can only be spoken of in faith, or in unfaith. But this does not mean that God is determined by our subjectivity. Rather it means that he is encountered in our historicity.

This might seem like an abandonment of God's alleged objectivity. But to try to maintain this objectivity is precisely what cannot be done with God. In the process of attempting this, you necessarily try to put him at a distance, to make him into an object of your attention—in other words, to make him a bit of yourself. God cannot be objectified. If you attempt to do this, you in fact do the opposite: you make him an extension of your subjectivity. But he can only be believed in your situation as the one who claims you, who invites you to accept his forgiveness, and to live by his grace.

'Claims'; 'forgives'; 'grace': where do I derive the right to introduce these ideas? Answer: from history: from the questions which man has always asked about the meaning of his life, and from the answer which comes in the historical approaches of God to man.

If you further ask, Where does he come from, then? And where may we turn to find him? I answer: look into your own history, look into that history of which your history (for you) is the concrete manifestation, and there you will be met.

To be met by God is not identical with any other encounter, whether with things or with human persons: but it is only in these encounters, in these temporal, spatial, relativized encounters, nowhere else, that God may be encountered. He is thoroughly involved in the human situation, he is absolutely for men. This at any rate is the message of the Judaeo-Christian faith, and it is consummated in Christ as his absolute Word.

Admittedly, this leaves the question of Being unanswered, except in the form of a new understanding of being, being as action, being as the creative Word, or, if you like, God's being-for-us. But this being-for-us is not Being either in the sense of the oldest tradition of all, as Heidegger calls it, that is, in the pre-socratic philosophers, or in the sense of the traditionalist concern with questions of entities.

This is, so far, not a very satisfactory conclusion, of course. To try to find a way between the thorough-going kenoticism of an unsophisticated and undialectical Jesu-centrism, as in Altizer (or in another form in van Buren), and the just as thorough-going ontologism of traditional theology, might well expose us to attack on two fronts. To the philosopher of being, who might well begin his questions by asking how I can possibly escape from using language of static and substantialist forms of thinking, so that even when I try to speak of the historicity of God I find myself speaking of his *being*-for-us, I can only reply that we are all under the dominance of that kind of language, and that particular grammar of being. Yet I must insist that the logic which I find in the historical Christian faith is a logic which is not static, but in movement. It is in movement in terms of history and historical experience. It is a *doing* to me which I am trying to understand, not a being simply. It is, if you like, not an ontology, but ginomenology.

One theologian has made a valiant effort to reconstitute traditional ways of theologizing in terms of a real and to a certain extent plausible critique of the tradition itself: I mean Karl Barth. The result is an extremely interesting combination of certain traditional elements with quite revolutionary turns to his thought. His solidly trinitarian starting-point, as I see it, attempts two things at once. First, it attempts to circumvent the whole traditional formulation of the question of being by an unremitting attack upon the so-called analogy of being. Natural theology has no place in Barth's theology. Then second, he introduces the conception of an *analogia relationis*, an analogy of relation. This promising start, however, becomes somewhat less promising when it becomes clear that for Barth this 'relation' is primarily the intra-trinitarian relation. You might ask, How does he get there? Certainly, he is tempted beyond bounds, as it seems to me, in his exposition of the intra-trinitarian mystery. But all the same, he clearly gets to this point by his unequivocal recognition that Christ is the event, *the* event, in which God's being is recognized in faith as being for us. But for Barth this event of Christ is, so to speak, sanctioned, guaranteed and in a sense objectified, in that it is acknowledged by faith to be the repetition of God's self-relation as Father, Son and Holy Spirit. God in Christ is so to speak the gloss upon God's being. Eberhard Jüngel, in developing this view in his essay on Barth's theology, *Gottes Sein ist im Werden* ('God's being is in becoming'), puts forward the suggestion that this means for Barth that God's hiddenness and his revealedness (in Christ) are, as relational being, a being in the power of becoming.[1]

In this way Barth, according to Jüngel, is still able to under-

---

[1] *op. cit.* p118.

stand God as being, but as gracious being. 'God's grace,' writes Jüngel, 'is the repetition of the "Yes" of God to himself in relation to another, which constitutes his being.'[1]

But in order to clinch the situation, that is, the ontological affirmation of God's being, Barth has to affirm in a quite direct manner that the becoming of God, that is, his 'Sein im Werden', his being in becoming in Christ, is not a becoming which passes away. This is affirmed in terms of belief in the Resurrection of Christ. Christ dies, but rises again. That is, he becomes, but his becoming is not simply a passing away, but a way of remaining.

Now it cannot be doubted that this is a grandiose effort to save the being of God. I cannot go with this enterprise. In other words, I cannot establish a doctrine of the Trinity in terms of a relational ontology standing by itself. I do not dispute the trinitarian necessity. But I can only point to what happens in history, and leave the question of the source of this happening in mystery. Or rather, the source of this happening is in the Word: but of the source of the Word nothing can be excogitated outside that Word that does not lead us into unprofitable speculations.

Here I must break off these preliminary reflections. Clearly, a theological anthropology must go about its business with more circumspection, yet without relinquishing the power of the mystery out of which everything comes to man.

I conclude with a few theses which, however cryptic as they stand, may serve for a provisional summary of the way that theology on my view will have to go:

(1) God moves through history.

(2) He approaches men through their history and no other way.

(3) Faith is the response to that movement.

(4) We may therefore talk about God when we turn to him

[1] *op. cit.* p118.

in our historical situation and talk to him—but always in the context of acknowledging our own incapacity to comprehend his utter grace.

(5) The whole world is open and waiting as the time and the place of the signature of that grace. We only need to recognize the writing which is interwoven in all history. There is no point at which the relation may not flare into a life of engagement.

(6) It is in this historical situation that transcendence re-emerges as a lived event, that is, as the presence of the Other.

(7) Further stages of the investigation clearly demand an analysis of temporality, and becoming, but no such analysis can be conducted in separation from the historical situation of man. This is the clear intention, and the merit, of Herbert Braun's description of God as 'das Woher meines Umgetriebenseins' ('the Whence of my being driven around').

(8) We can only say of God what he does to us.

VIII

How does God act?

This question, How does God act? can be taken as a touchstone by which a variety of possible modern attitudes may be tested. So it is a crucial question. The answer that you give to it decides just what your relation to Christianity is. I want to try and clarify the attitudes that seem to me to be current. Then you can judge for yourselves which attitude is the most comprehensive and realistic for you.

I can detect three main attitudes, though of course I shall have to simplify them so much that they do not necessarily correspond to the mixture, even the confusion, of views which are often found to be residing in one individual's attitude.

The first main attitude is what I should call the naïve traditional view. It may be illustrated by an old formula which is still to be read occasionally in the railway stations of Britain. The railways in the course of their history developed a complicated series of regulations. They were particularly anxious to define and circumscribe their responsibilities, the limit to their responsibilities, regarding the passengers and goods which they carried. And so they listed a great many contingencies which exempted them from their normal responsibility. Thus tempest and flood, wars and riots, were events for which they refused to accept responsibility. But included in this list was also something which was described as 'an act of God'.

This act of God was not further defined. But in the context I think we can see approximately how it was regarded. It was regarded as something similar to natural or national calamities, as something over which no one, at least no one in the railway company, had any control. It was even more arbitrary than a riot or a flood or a war, since it broke in upon the orderly sequence of events, the shining lines of the railway, the punctual trains, the ordered progress from one station to the next, as an act which just could not be explained within the ordinary sequence at all. It was a wonderful escape clause for the railways, since it really included anything that might happen which they could not possibly foresee.

I do not know whether any action brought against a railway company was ever successfully defended in terms of this clause about an act of God. If it had been, then we might have obtained an interesting insight into nineteenth-century popular theology.

But besides the element of arbitrariness in this view, there is another presupposition, and this also is found in the heart of the naïve traditional theology about acts of God. It is the presupposition that the act of God, while arbitrary, and surprising, and even confounding the ordinary run of things, in nature and history, can also be seen, discerned, and understood, in much the same way as ordinary events and actions. Because it is regarded as God's act, it is of course also admitted to be extraordinary. But in so far as it is observable as in some way or other fitting into the natural chain of events it is in fact being given the same status as other, natural events. This fact is concealed, usually, by its being described as having a different status. For instance, one normal way of describing an act of God, on this naïve traditional view, is to speak of it as being due to a supernatural cause. But this use of the term 'supernatural' does not succeed in removing the conception of the act of God from the sphere of natural events. Somehow it is fitted into the sphere of nature, as an extra link in the chain, or as a miracle which cannot but be noticed, sticking out of the ordinary sequence of events as something done not by man but by God. But the arbitrary and extraordinary elements have in fact been replaced by a rational description which has made the act of God just a bit of nature.

In the context of biblical history this view has been developed, especially in the nineteenth century, in the course of the struggle of religious ideas with the views of modern science. It has been refined in our time, and is to be found, for instance, in the fashionable work of the Swiss theologian, Oscar Cullmann, *Christ and Time*.[1] In that work the view of *Heilsgeschichte*, or redemptive history, is worked out in terms of a highly simplified and very attractive picture of biblical history, which runs somewhat as follows. Cullmann regards God's action of redemption as taking place in the sequence of events along the line of time. It began in the breadth of universal human history, and then was narrowed down through the selection, and then the rejection, of Israel to what Cullmann calls the mid-point, as it were the burning-point, of all history, namely, Christ, to broaden out again from him through the Church to the universal fulfilment in the parousia or coming-again of Christ.[2] This simplified version of redemptive history is described as a series of momentous happenings, mighty moments, which are objectively discernible in the history of the world, and especially in the history of Israel, of Christ, and of the Church. Thus the call of Abraham, the giving of the law on Mt Sinai, the Exodus, the Return, the development of the idea of the remnant of Israel, then Christ as the mid-point, solitary, the one remaining member of Israel, are each in turn seen as mighty acts of God, as his acts which are now revealed or disclosed, open to the world, and bearing within them, as it were, the real meaning of all history.

---

[1] S.C.M. Press, London 1962 (revised ed.) and Westminster Press, Philadelphia 1964 (revised ed.).
[2] Cf. a fuller treatment of the theme of 'Heilsgeschichte' in my *Secular Christianity*, Collins, London and Harper and Row, New York, 1966 pp107*ff*.

This view of God's acts rests entirely upon the nineteenth-century positivist view of history, as a collection of facts which can be pointed to and which are supposed to bear their own meaning in themselves. This meaning, of course, is extended in the sense that it is regarded as part of an evolution or steady progress towards a given goal. God's acts are thus conceived of as somehow running parallel and being analogous to world-historical events. And the man who believes in God's acts in this way is regarded as a man who subscribes to this view of events, who looks at them and acknowledges that they have occurred in this way and for this purpose. He stands outside the stream of history, he is on the bank of the river and sees how things are flowing, he enters the stream only like a passenger embarking on a ship, and that is the extent of his participation. He is made a passenger on the ship of the divine acts.

In all this the question of the ambiguity of the chosen events themselves, and the question of the rest of history, is silently suppressed. It is by an immense operation of simplification that this view of how God acts is kept before the mind of the ordinary conventional believer. No wonder that he is sometimes uneasy. And that he often takes himself off from this kind of view. For as a rule this view claims to be the necessary concomitant of Christian faith.

So we come to the second possible attitude to the question of how God acts. It is simply the attitude that decides that there is no meaning in the question at all. Or rather, it is an outdated mythology which is at work here. This attitude may again be greatly varied. It may contain an element of true and reverent agnosticism. It may be that there is a God, it may be that if there is a God he is somehow working upon his creation, if it is his creation and not the already formed work of a hostile god. But in this agnosticism no answer to such questions can be given. For how may a mere passing human, with his fragmentary

127

knowledge about a mysterious universe, venture to draw into this world any talk about an act of God?

I must confess that I prefer this agnosticism to the blithe assurance in the traditional view that as it were has God taped, and has removed the mystery from his being.

And when this second view lays more stress upon the negations than upon the mystery, here too I must confess that I find the attitude more congenial than the traditional view. Here we are really dealing with the basic presupposition of ordinary secular modern man, the presupposition that this world must somehow stand on its own feet, that the reference to another, transcendent world, or to an other-worldly metaphysic, simply does not mean anything, and that, indeed, the world has meaning in itself, or, if it does not have, cannot be given meaning from outside at all. Such a modern man if pressed would admit that there is something attractive in the thought of a superhuman fatherly figure looking after everything, in much the way that a human father looks after his children, only infinitely more so. But his trouble is that this just looks to him like an unwarranted mythology. And what content can be put into the conception of 'infinitely more so'? The modern man of whom I am thinking rightly rejects the first traditional view as being meaningless to his situation. He rightly rejects a mythology which allows God's act or acts to be regarded as an intervention between the ordinary events of the world. (I recall a malicious story of Aldous Huxley in which a missionary was travelling in a train in order to address a church gathering. He was told by his fellow-travellers that the train did not stop at the station he wished to get out at. But the missionary prayed. Then as the train approached his station he got up and prepared to get out. Sure enough, the train slowed up and finally drew to a halt at the station, and the missionary descended. The train had in fact stopped because the man who was coming to meet the missionary had crossed the level-crossing in his car, or rather had tried to cross, just as the earlier express train was coming through. The car and its driver were of course destroyed, but the missionary got through to his meeting in good time.)

But we are not left with the choice between simple credulity and complex agnosticism. There is a third attitude, and this is the one I wish to place before you as being more adequate to the reality of Christian faith than the others. This view, like the agnostic view, has also a strong sense of the mystery of the universe. This sense is concentrated in the view that the action of God is always hidden. That is to say, it is not simply and directly observable and demonstrable as true in the same way as other happenings are observable and demonstrable. It is hidden 'from every eye except the eye of faith'.[1] It cannot be objectified in the world, for it is an act proceeding from the one who is simply not of this world. He is, as Kierkegaard, but not only Kierkegaard, has said, 'qualitatively different' from the world. I say 'not only Kierkegaard', for the tradition of negative theology coming from the Middle Ages, but also with its roots in the biblical view of faith, has elaborated a whole system of negations about God. These negations are intended to preserve the mystery of the hiddenness of God's being. You cannot speak directly of God as being in the world. You cannot see him at work. You cannot demonstrate that here and here he was demonstrably present. You cannot prove any of the convictions of faith in the way that you can prove that any ordinary natural or historical happening has taken place. You are here moving in the realm of faith, and this is the only realm in which you may properly speak of God.

Yet even in the realm of faith you cannot speak of God as he is. This means that you cannot construct a system which is so openly consistent that it bears the possibility of being verified by

[1]Rudolf Bultmann *Jesus Christ and Mythology* S.C.M. Press, London 1960 and Scribner's, New York 1958 p62.

the canons of the world. You can only speak in faith of his acts as taking place within the life of the world.

What does this mean, to speak in faith of God's acts? It means that the mystery of God's otherness is not removed. It remains a mystery. It means that God's act is a paradox. It unites within itself the ordinary actions of the world with God's loving will for the world. So it means that in each event which comes into your life you are invited, or if you like you are challenged, to respond to this event as one in which simultaneously with its everyday meaning you recognize and acknowledge that here God is at work. This does not mean that you replace the ordinary meaning of the event with a divine meaning. But it means that in this event, within it, not destroying it, you acknowledge that God is present.

Does this mean that faith is simply a will to believe? A wish on your part, a subjectivist desire that there should be a God? Not at all. But it does mean that your belief in the reality of God's act is an essential part of the situation. Your faith grows out of the substance of your personal life regarded as historical. It is not enough for you to look at the biblical records as from the outside, to accept certain propositions about them, not even the propositions about God's mighty acts, and then to subscribe to them as your belief. This is a subordinate view of belief which is not the basic view. The basic view of faith is one in which you yourself enter into the relation of trust. 'All faith is passion and risk', as Paul Tillich has said. You have to take the step, which is a risk, that God is actually acting in relation to you and your own life.

Now I have not yet said anything about the meaning of God's act in Christ, but I hope that it has already become clear that this has been implicit in the whole analysis. God's act in Christ partakes pre-eminently of that paradoxical nature of which I have spoken. Here you have the simple historical facts, the life-story of Jesus of Nazareth, in which, within which, resides simultaneously God's challenge to your existence. That is to say, you are invited to believe that God is here, in Christ, acting once for all on behalf of men. You are invited to believe that here is the paradox, the judgement on all history, on all life, including your own life, and at the same time the invitation to a new world, a new life. If you wish to retain the conception of the 'redemptive story', *Heilsgeschichte*, then you may do so in terms of this life of Christ. He is the only *Heilsgeschichte*, the redemptive act of God. But not in the traditional view. For he does not become visible as the best or the supreme illustrator of the series of divine actions. On the contrary, he is present to faith as the one who makes an end of all old-fashioned *Heilsgeschichte*, all 'boasting'. In his life and death he judges and puts an end to all human self-assertion. There is no hope in the history of the world, as such. Indeed, there is no meaning in the history of the world as such. The only meaning you can find is what is put into it by the redemptive story of Christ. The meaning that is in the once-for-all coming of Christ is a meaning that is to be found by you here and now in your own decision to put your life into his care. This is the Word of God, namely, as you encounter it in the midst of your own life's history.

So the act of God remains hidden, it remains entirely personal, it is incapable of proof, incapable of demonstration, a mystery and indeed an offence and a stumbling-block to ordinary means of excogitation and analysis. But it is none the less the reality by which faith lives, and it is only by faith that you may live with the proper balance in this world, a world by itself without meaning, and rushing towards death and nothingness, and at the same time a world which can be restored by that same faith to the status of God's creation, and you may be restored to the status of a son within that creation.

IX

The Resurrection of Christ

The Resurrection of Christ is not in the first instance an intellectual problem which has been set for theologians to try and solve. It is a reality in the midst of history. The concomitant elements in the New Testament record which point to this reality are indeed many and various. But in spite of these complications the heart of this reality is simple. From man's side, that is, from his response of faith, the simplicity can best be expressed, and is historically expressed, as joy and assurance.

Even if you cannot find your way through the complications, you are still able to come out of your own isolation. Christian faith is not a matter of passing an examination in the items adjudged orthodox. But it is a decision for the new life of freedom which awaits you in the joy of God.

> 'For indeed dreary and petty, oppressive and imprisoning, is our poor little life, on its surface and apart from God and His merciful condescensions towards us. But we would not know our misery, we would not feel it as such, were there not Saints and Heroes around us, and Christ our Lord above us, and, encompassing all and penetrating all, God— not a Sufferer, but indeed the Sympathiser, God Joy, the Ocean of Joy, our Home.'[1]

Without this joy, of which von Hügel speaks, from God to man, there is nothing to talk about.

The disputations of theologians, however, need not be a mere academic game. They are able to help us to understand our faith.

[1]Friedrich von Hügel *Essays and Addresses* Dent, London 1928 Vol II p213.

This is not the place to attempt a whole theology of the Resurrection. In any case, it is axiomatic that you cannot isolate the Resurrection from the life and death of Christ. I wish to give here just a few pointers to the way in which we must approach the theological issues.

Generally speaking, today, theological discussion of the Resurrection revolves round a few unexamined presuppositions of thought. These presuppositions concern certain ways of regarding Scripture, a specific epistemology and metaphysic.

In regard to Scripture, the basic point at issue is how we understand its varied style and its differing accounts. In brief, we have to recognize that our modern understanding of events of the past is both more complex and clearer than that even of the writers of the New Testament. Past events *qua* past events are accessible to us only as approximations. We cannot rest our faith upon probabilities which cannot be verified. But beyond the disputable reconstructions of past events there is another access: in terms of the present, of the demand made upon us to believe or to reject, the past rises up, as it were, to confront us. The event of the life and death and resurrection of Christ confronts us in the tradition of the Church. We are faced by it in every presentation of the story. In particular, every Sunday, which in its origin was a celebration of the Easter story, we are at liberty to hear this story and meet its demand upon us. That is to say, we may encounter this demand if the traditional means—the celebration of the sacrament, the hearing of Scripture, the preaching of the Word—have not been overlaid by extraneous material or otherwise stifled.

The demand laid upon us by the Easter story cannot be reduced to a demand to believe in the empty tomb, or in the physical, observable, and demonstrable reanimation of a dead person. Nor can it be reduced to the demand to accept as central the legends and embellishments of which even the canonical Gospels are full. It needs a decided effort of the his-

133

torical and literary imagination to think oneself into the world-view of the original shapers of these beautiful stories. But faith does not consist in the strength of our imagination.

In regard to the specific epistemology with which theologians normally work today, the issues at stake are alleged to revolve round questions of 'facts' and 'objective events' on the one hand, and 'interpretations of facts' and 'subjective experiences' on the other hand. This epistemology is highly sophisticated. It is not to be found in the New Testament. It is not even generally accepted today.

Nor again is the metaphysic of two spheres—the sphere of the natural and the sphere of the supernatural—intrinsic to the reality of New Testament faith. The chief and crucial distinction in the New Testament way of thinking is rather between death and life, between the old creation and the new creation, between the old aeon which is passing away and the new aeon which has come in Christ. This is an *eschatological* view of life, and at the heart of it is the faith that Christ himself is the Last One.

The decisive point here is that we in our present lives may be confronted by the reality of Christ in such a way that we may enter into a new life. This reality is not simply his Resurrection, but is his whole historical reality. The Resurrection is not just a triumphant addition to the sorry or tragic story of the life and death of Christ. It is not a *bouleversement* of all that went before it. It is not an act of *force majeure* on the part of God. God does not write off all that went before, by means of an action which bears no conceivable relation to all the previous story. If this were the reality of the Resurrection, then we should be committing ourselves to the acceptance of an action which is sheerly unhistorical, and therefore nonsense.

To attempt to evade this charge, theologians have invented ways of describing the Resurrection as being 'beyond history', or 'supra-historical', yet impinging upon history. They are at this point inviting us to abandon all conception of history as real.

Basically, they are asking for belief in a docetic Christ, that is, one who never was really and truly man, that is, fully historical.

If the objection is made that such views indicate the unavoidable stumbling-block in Christianity, and that we must be ready to sacrifice our understanding, then I can only reply that this seems to me to miss the mark. I am not being invited to accept a message which simply ignores the way of Christ in the world, which was the way of powerless love. But I am being invited to accept forgiveness for what I have been, and invited to enter into a life of joyful and assured faith. This I cannot do in the terms supplied by many modern apologists, who seek to keep alive out-of-date and irrelevant modes of thought about history.

We are not asked to believe in the empty tomb. We are not even asked to believe in an isolated fact entitled 'the Resurrection'. Christian faith does not lean upon such so-called 'facts' of history. The real dimension of Christian faith, however, is so thoroughly historical that it takes in the whole reality of Christ, past, present and future. And this is why we are not asked to believe in the Resurrection as an alleged item of history.

But we are asked to believe in the living Lord. This is the same belief as the disciples themselves exhibited in the first days of the Easter faith. They believed because they believed in his life and death as the forgiving action of God.

The real *skandalon* or stumbling-block, then, is not that we are asked to accept as a verifiable piece of 'history' an anti-historical dramatic intervention of God in the form of a miraculous objective act, namely the raising from the dead. But the *skandalon* is that we are invited to believe that here in the life and death of a man God has entered into man's historical existence and in this life and death has acted out his own being, as a being-for-men, and not against them. This means that the Resurrection may be seen as the way in which God acts his forgiveness of men. Thus to believe in the Resurrection means to believe that

135

God affirms his forgiving purpose in the historical reality of the life of Christ.

Perhaps it may still be said that while denying that the Resurrection is an accessible historical fact in the sense of an irrefragable argument based upon irrefragable evidence, such as the empty tomb, the appearances to the disciples, and the like, I am still ready to talk about the Resurrection as a mysterious reality. And might it not be said that my attempt to abandon the historical proof of the Resurrection is as obscurantist as the traditional desire to maintain this proof? After all, what *is* the Resurrection if it is not God's mightiest of all miracles? And who am I to gainsay God's omnipotence?

Who am I? I am just another of those same obscure people who like everyone else is more or less conscious of the futility of his existence, and of how it is rushing towards death. At the same time I recognize that in the history of Christ I am offered a new way of existence: I am not after all given over to myself, bound hand and foot by my own past, and the past which I have inherited from the mass of death that has made my life possible. I am given the chance of being renewed. And this renewal, so far as my faith reaches, faith which is no sight, and only in a special sense knowledge—and partial at that—is possible only through the recognition and the acceptance of the sheer goodness of God. But it is a goodness which, in the circumstances of the case—that is, the case of man's implication in his own historical fate—does not work by direct application of power. It works only by the same suffering love which is the gift of Christ. This suffering love may be joyfully affirmed to be all-conquering. But it is so only to faith.

X

Faith in a Secular World

1

*The popular view of faith and of secularism,
and the consequent opposition between the two,
or the irrelevance of the one to the other*

What is the relation of Christianity and modern secularism?
This is a question which sounds to many people, both simple
believers and simple secularists, like an attempt to bring together two disparate entities: entities which belong to different
worlds of thought and of living. And the attempt therefore
seems to such people necessarily to end either in the opposition
of faith to secularism (if you are a believer) or in the indifference
of secularism to faith (if you are a secularist). Of course it is
possible for there to be an uneasy co-existence in the life of one
and the same man of both the concern of faith and the concern
of secularism, for instance in the life of a scientist who says his
prayers but who does not allow his research and his prayers to
affect one another in any way. But this means in effect the
gradual elimination of the concern of faith from the empirical
everyday world in which modern secularized man goes about
his real business.

This popular view both of faith and of secularism, that the
two are at bottom irreconcilable because they are necessarily
concerned with different realities, has been so often expressed
that I need only remind you of two typical remarks. The theologians here will know of the great conference of the Inter-

137

national Missionary Council held in Jerusalem in 1928, when the American Quaker, Rufus M. Jones, the president of the conference, defined secularism as 'a way of life and an interpretation of life that include only the natural order of things and that do not find God, or a realm of spiritual reality, essential for life and thought':[1] a way of life, therefore, that he regarded as 'a vast unconquered rival of Christianity'. The second typical remark was made by Pastor Niemoeller to Adolf Hitler, on the 25th January, 1934: 'You have said, "Leave me to care for the German people." I must tell you that neither you nor any power in the world is in a position to take from us, as Christians and Church, the responsibility for our people that has been laid upon us by God.'

Although a generation has passed since these remarks were made, the popular view has not changed. And it is supported by weighty arguments on both sides.

This popular view, so far as faith is concerned, rests upon the acceptance of a specific world-picture which has its sources deep in traditional theology. It is a theistic view, certainly, in so far as it carries with it the necessary implication of the existence of God. On this view, therefore, the question does not arise whether possibly the necessary implication that there is a God does not itself in the end imply the destruction of faith, and indeed a basically atheist view of life. I mean that to suggest that God is, as a necessary implication and therefore precondition and pre-givenness of faith, is itself an atheist assertion. But this popular view which I am describing can make nothing of such a suggestion. For this view posits and presupposes a world-picture in which there is a natural and a supernatural realm. On the one hand there is the present this-worldly world in which we live and work and plan and make our researches and

[1]The Jerusalem Meeting of the International Missionary Council 1928, I, p230.

advances by specific and verifiable steps into our own controlled future. And on the other hand there is the world in which faith operates, a realm which claims to complete and perfect the realm of nature. The language of this realm is quite different from the language of the natural realm. Its realities are derived from events which in a remarkable way are claimed to be both historical and suprahistorical at the same time. They are salvation events, *Heilsgeschichte*, which is both history in the ordinary sense and yet superior to ordinary history. These events overarch the ordinary historical world with a claim both to judge and to explain the ordinary world. This claim is elaborated in a system of doctrines which has hitherto endeavoured—and indeed with considerable success through the centuries of Christendom—to meet the needs both of individuals and of society, and to lift men and society above the threat of meaninglessness and to hold them, as it were, uneasily yet in comparative security above the transient and perishing natural world. In this view the Church is then regarded as an ark which rescues men from the floods of time, and offers them the security of eternity.

But to the secularized man of today these claims are either regarded as hostile to his own sense of what is important, or else, more commonly, as irrelevant. The language of otherworldliness sounds not merely archaic to him, it also has a whiff of arbitrariness about it, in that it seems to him to ignore the empirical actualities of his ordinary life. Transcendence of the kind that is implied in this view of faith does not seem to him to apply to his life. For in effect modern secularized man has lost the sense of transcendence, at least as it is given in the traditional doctrines of Christianity. I do not know if we can say that he has lost the feeling for the numinous, or what I should call the sense of reverence before the utter givenness of life. On the whole, however, I think it is fair to say that if the ordinary unreflective man of today does have a passion for goodness or a

139

love of beauty or a reverence for truth, he understands these things in terms of his own entirely self-sufficient world, the world of co-humanity in the one world that he knows. It is an entirely relativized and pluralistic world in which he lives, and its advancement and enhancement lie, on his view, entirely within the realm of the planned choices which are available to him.

I have put the two sides of the matter crudely, and clearly there are qualifications and modifications in each individual of the two extreme views. The man who holds by the traditional view of faith does not simply live in heaven, nor even in a cata-comb of the spirit; but at the very least he makes sporadic and uneasy forays into the empirical world—indeed, he usually may be found to live at least partly (sometimes from Mondays to Saturdays *entirely*) in the secular world. And on the other hand the secular man, who wishes to run his own life, is sometimes appalled by the immense powers which he himself has liberated, and turns in anguish to some external support: it may be a political party, it may be some good cause, such as a campaign for disarmament, or the helping of the hungry in the world. In turning to such a cause such a man is looking, usually un-consciously, for a substitute for the transcendent world which he has lost.

2

The real nature of faith

But behind the accepted and popular views both of faith and of secularism there lies a much more complicated story. It is in-deed a story of relation and mutuality. This story can be analyzed from many different angles, sociological, phenomenological, and more broadly as the history of the human spirit. But the basic single and uniting aspect for seeing the real relation of faith and secularism is the complex aspect which I should call the theological-historical. It is on a view of the full historicity of faith, and the consequent entire historicity of man's destiny, that faith and secularism may be seen to be not enemies, and not indifferent rivals, but partners, and, as I hope to show, partners who are absolutely indispensable the one to the other. Certainly, in showing this, I have also to show how our understanding of both entities, both faith and secularism, must undergo a transformation. The popular view is inadequate for both of them.

First of all, faith. Faith is not primarily a doctrine or teaching about life which is based upon a specific world-view. Nor on the other hand is faith simply a withdrawal into inwardness. Faith cannot be adequately comprehended within categories which imply a subject-object schema: faith is neither a doctrine concerning objects nor simply a subjective experience. Faith is rather to be seen as arising in a thoroughly historical context. Faith arises as the consequence of specific, particular, human historical events, and it continues in its essential life-form to be determined by these events. These events are concentrated in the life, death and resurrection of Christ. But we do not merely draw from these events certain doctrines about man's life in relation to God and to the world. Of course, there is a place for doctrine, and therefore for a certain kind of objectivity. But the traditional dogmatic teaching makes itself merely burdensome when it attempts to put into the centre a normative teaching which is supposed to be identical with faith.[1] This is what has happened again and again in the history of theology and of the Church. What I am now suggesting, instead of this procedure, is not merely that you accept another and new structure of

[1]Cf. W. Herrmann 'Christlich-Protestantische Dogmatik' 2nd ed. 1909, in *Schriften zur Grundlegung der Theologie*, I, 1966 pp342*ff*.

normative teaching. What I am suggesting is both simpler, and harder: it is that we try to understand faith on its own terms, that is, in terms of how it has really come to be, how it has arisen. And about the basic nature of this coming-to-be I suggest there can be no doubt: faith has always arisen as the response to historical events. And its very essence is determined by these events, so that without them faith would either become simply gnosis, a way of knowing about the world and God and yourself, or it would become just an arbitrary perspective on life suitable to some temperaments and not to others. But faith is the response to the message concerning Christ, and this message comes entirely as a historical address and demand. The believer is one who recognizes in this message the end of the old world, of death and judgement, and the simultaneous beginning of a new world. But the new world is not less historical than the old world. On the contrary, it is more fully historical than any other world. For the believer, while being taken out of the old world, is simultaneously put back into the world. This is the heart of what is meant by that strange and much-disputed word 'eschatology'. In the message concerning Christ there really is an end to the old—the old self-justification, the old fears, the old being-enclosed by a world of fate, the old threat of meaninglessness, the old tendency to turn again and again to a world of gods, who are real enough, but are not more than powerful objects within the world. There is an end to all this. But at the same time there is a new beginning. It is a beginning in faith, of course: faith is the power which responds to the call for newness, and for a new kind of love and hope. But this new beginning means in fact, in simple empirical fact, a new relation both to God and to the world. It means a new binding to God and a new freedom for the world.

Clearly, on this view, a new conception of the world and of history is also implied. It is a conception of the world as being both given by God and created by man. Man is the secondary creator. He makes the world what God wants it to be. He makes it into the realm of his, man's historical destiny. The world is no longer a fate overshadowing, overarching him, but is now the open theatre of his destiny. And this implies a conception of history which is different from the traditional conception. The historical events which provide the challenge to which faith is the response cannot be conceived of simply as static entities residing in an utterly past, dead-and-gone world. The eschatological reality of the event of Christ, in particular, means that it is not simply part of the dead-and-gone past. On the contrary, the view of history which is here necessarily implied is that this eschatological reality forms part of the possibility of our present history now. Even more, it is the determinative reality of our present history. Eschatology does not mean a doctrine concerning an indeterminate future, when time will be wound up: but it means the present reality of a demand upon me now, which awaits my decision in faith. History, therefore, may be described as the field of human decisions, or more precisely as my personal acting in making my world into the world which God desires of me. History is therefore my present act. It is therefore faith which makes possible truly secular and historical action now.

In Gogarten's words, 'history is the presentness of the past'.[1] The eschatological reality of Christ's historical being, however, is not thereby equated with what has been called 'a realized eschatology'. In principle, yes: the end has come in Christ. But also, paradoxically, this end is not yet: we live now in the time of God's patience with his world, in which by faith we may continually overcome the old world and live towards the new. In this sense there is a real future, which is now recognized by faith as the future which God offers, in the complete humanity which he has already offered in Christ.

[1]Friedrich Gogarten *Ich glaube an den dreieinigen Gott* Diederichs, Jena 1926 p19.

I do not intend here to draw out all kinds of doctrines from this basic position, although it is clear that doctrines have to be drawn out for the sake always of a fuller understanding of faith itself. What I wish to emphasize here is that this view of the eminent historicity of faith is not itself a doctrine or even a world-picture which I am trying to impose upon the material of faith. But this historicity of faith is the very way in which faith exists. To talk about faith as historical, therefore, is to talk about its essential reality, and as it were to draw out of faith the very power which resides in it.

If all this is essentially true of faith, then we have the beginnings of a very different perspective upon secularism. But before we look more closely at what faith's responsibility in and for the world must mean today, let us turn to what secularism in itself appears to mean.

3

The real nature of secularism

I forbear to give any detailed account of the rise of secularism in Europe. There are many delineations of the process, and as you might expect there is nearly always a polemical tone in the descriptions. This is to be expected just because secularization is a living actuality in our midst. What is going on in every sphere of society today is an increasing secularization. The whole of society is rapidly developing an immense and immensely rich manifoldness, and the various specialized and more or less autonomous disciplines in a modern university are merely the academic reflection of a movement which is to be seen throughout society. This state of affairs has reached its present point by means of a progressive liberation of human affairs from the bondage of a certain doctrine about the world—the doctrine which I have already described as the twofold view of the natural and the supernatural, which implies of course both a specific metaphysic and a specific style of life in terms of the sacred and the profane.

It is customary to speak of the beginnings of this movement of emancipation as occurring at the Renaissance, but it is hard to determine with any clarity just when this movement towards the autonomy of man's interests took its rise. In another sense the *Aufklärung* of the eighteenth century is the point of self-conscious and critical recognition of what is happening. From the *Aufklärung* our society has developed in a more or less continuous line. For it was in the *Aufklärung* that there arose more clearly than ever before the conception of the autonomy of human reason. Not, please note, the simple autonomy of man, but the autonomy of his reason in dealing with his whole inherited traditions, religious, political, and moral. In every sphere of man's life this ever-more-autonomous reason replaced the old sacral bonds with an empirical and matter-of-fact analysis of the possibilities inherent in the situation itself. As Martin Stallmann says, it was in the eighteenth century that secularization became a 'usable political concept, when political power was thoroughly established as a worldly power'.[1] But today secularization in the negative sense of emancipation from sacral orders has proliferated into every area of human activity. And at the same time this proliferation has produced certain limited but indubitable positive gains for man: rational criticism of every received doctrine, whether in science or medicine or sociology or law or politics, has made possible the immense technological and social advances of our era, and makes possible the attitude of provisionalness and openness to every acknowledged gain. 'The world's my oyster which with sword I'll open,' as Pistol said in *The Merry Wives of Windsor*. The sword

[1] *Was ist Säkularisierung?* J. C. B. Mohr (Paul Siebeck), Tübingen 1960.

with which modern secular man opens his world is the sword of his autonomous reason. Nothing is withheld from the possibility of exploration and re-assessment. Nothing is sacred any more.

Moreover, if anything should go wrong in this controlled manipulation of nature and of human history, modern man is not essentially thrown off balance by this. This kind of mishap he simply regards as an error which must be corrected, and which can be corrected. Perhaps we shall be unlucky, and perhaps the whole of our society will be engulfed in an atomic disaster. But the way to deal with this threat is to plan our relationships all the more carefully. The whole new science of cybernetics is intended to govern and guide human decisions towards the enhancement of human togetherness, and towards the elimination of sub-human drives.

What is the positive expectation of this controlled manipulation? It is by no means slight. I should give it the general description of co-humanity. An ever-increasing co-humanity, in tolerance for differing views, in care for the unlucky and for the underdeveloped nations: an enhancement of the possibilities of each individual's life, within the context established by the general welfare. If I were putting this expectation as positively as I can, I should call it the development of human possibilities within the limits set by man's own powers: and tacitly these limits are not even bounded by death: for death is not an essential ingredient of the expectations of secular man. If I were putting the expectation in a more critical form, I should say it is the expectation that men themselves are self-creative, and that God as the creator, the giver, the beginning and the end, as the Limit to human aspiration, has been replaced by man.

More modestly, however, I think that the actual truth of the present state of affairs must be set somewhere between these two extremes. For secularism regarded as an inevitable process suffers in truth today from a certain malaise. And this malaise arises from the fact, which cannot be controverted by any optimistic assessment of man's powers, that in the actual working-out of man's destiny, in his freely-chosen possibilities, there is one significant and far-reaching fault. It is that in this intensely exciting manipulation of man's future man as man tends to drop out of the centre of the picture. Man as man means for me in the first instance man as the single person with his personal world, man not merely as an item in the forward march of humanity, but man as an end in himself. We can see this deep fault when we look as spectators at the way in which the aims of a Marxist society ride roughshod over the actual living present single person. The co-humanity has been postponed till a later day. This means that in truth the co-humanity has become an abstraction in the service of an ideology. But in a similar way we must say that the whole of our society is so much under the threat of what I have called controlled manipulation that co-humanity is everywhere becoming a mere abstraction. So man as man is flattened out. He loses his personal being. And it does not basically help if he is treated by the welfare state in his particular needs, whether of mind or soul or body: he is still not a Thou, but just an It. And with this accusation I rest the case against modern secularism, and return to the question of the real relation between faith and secularism. What does faith mean in this secularized world?

4

The necessity of faith for the maintenance of true secularity

As I see the state of affairs today, the trouble with modern secularism is that it is not secular enough. It does not have the courage of its own origins. Its origins, as I have already indicated, lie within the freedom given by faith, which involves a free bond to God and a free responsibility for the world. Without a constant acknowledgement of these origins, and a constant criticism of its own enterprises and aims by means of these origins, secularism is bound to fail. That is, it is bound to fail if it does not recognize the dialectic inherent in its own processes. This dialectic is not a doctrine, nor an abstraction. It is a historical reality. By historical reality I mean quite simply that a true secularity puts man absolutely at the centre of the world. This does not mean that man in his co-humanity is the whole of reality. But it means that man's co-humanity can only be safeguarded and promoted by means of the recognition that everything has been given to him. Man's task as secular man depends upon the gift of his humanity. His co-humanity is therefore in truth an inter-humanity. It is not in the individual himself that we find the reality of man. But neither can we find this reality in an abstraction, say, humanity, which demands that the individual subordinate himself to it. Man as man is a possibility only in terms of a more thorough-going secularity than our modern secularism has so far displayed. And this more thorough-going secularity is only possible by means of the insights and the power of faith. In other words, it is only by an acknowledgement of faith in God that the historical reality of man can be authentically forwarded.

But what is meant here by the word 'God'? Am I after all suggesting a repristination of the old teachings? Is the solution to the malaise of modern secularism simply that the Christian believer, and the Church of which he is a part, should freshen up the old proclamation, and so rescue individuals from the naughty world and set them sailing down the river of time in a safely insulated ark? I suggest that a proper confession of what we mean by God should send us out in a different way into the world which we share with everyone else. The thought of God is certainly the most heavily-laden, but also the most promising, of all our inheritance. But the way to understand this tradition is assuredly not easy or simple.

The difficulty may be seen when we consider the lively activity noticeable in America today. In the USA the development of secularism has reached proportions not yet known in Europe or elsewhere. Just for that reason the problem has reached more outrageous forms than elsewhere. On the one hand there is the tidal wave of religiosity, which has, they say, to some extent subsided. On the other hand there are the so-called death-of-God theologians. These theologians have recently been described by Karl Barth as young fellows who are just exponents of *Unkultur*. But they cannot be so easily disposed of. For their problem is precisely the problem of how to live as truly human persons with on the one hand a Christian tradition which is basically uncertain of its relation to this world, and on the other hand with a world which they instinctively—and as I believe rightly—wish to affirm. How can a Christian believer affirm a world in which God has dropped out of the picture?

The responses of these American theologians are very varied. I cannot say that I am satisfied with any of them. Gabriel Vahanian is content to indicate with a wealth of example that modern man is essentially living in a post-Christian world, a world which is completely immanentist, and his remedy for this state of affairs is a return to obedience to the God conceived of as utterly different from this world.[1] Van Buren, on the other hand, is ready to eliminate all talk of God as meaningless, and to find his inspiration in the life of Jesus. Jesus is the free man who makes others free. The result for him is a lofty Christian humanism, in which the whole possibility of transcendence has been jettisoned.[2] Altizer is of a different temper. In his *Gospel of*

[1] Cf. G. Vahanian *The Death of God*, 1961; *Wait without idols*, 1964; and *No other God*, 1966, Braziller, New York
[2] Cf. Paul van Buren *The Secular Meaning of the Gospel* S.C.M. Press, London and Macmillan Co., New York 1963.

Christian Atheism[1] he proposes a view of Christianity which takes utterly radically the death of God. This goes much further than Nietzsche whose notorious affirmation of the death of God was, it seems to me—and here I follow Heidegger—simply the assertion of the end of a certain way of thinking about God: essentially the god of Greek philosophy. But for Altizer the Christian faith means the recognition of the complete self-emptying of God into Christ. There is no other god than what we have in Christ. And Christ is dead, so God is dead. But Christ has risen into human history. So we partake in our historical development of the utter incarnation of God in Christ. So God is to be found in the working-out of human history and human possibilities. Here too transcendence has been jettisoned.

I consider that none of these attempts to pinpoint God, and to make room for God in the story of man, succeeds in penetrating to the heart of the problem. The heart of the problem is how we regard Christ. To put the matter theologically, it is a christological problem which faces us here. But to put the problem in terms of secular man, it is a human problem which faces us. How may we understand Christ as being really involved in the human secular problems of our time? If we cannot answer this question in concrete actual terms then we are bound to fall back on the traditional dichotomy, and to affirm Christ at the expense of the world (if we are believers), or to affirm the world at the expense of Christ (if we are simply secularist). But we are asking about the possibility of an entirely historical God.

[1]T. J. J. Altizer *The Gospel of Christian Atheism* Collins, London and Westminster Press, Philadelphia 1967.

5

Tentative conclusions

My own answer to this question is only tentative. It involves a view of the reality of God which is not congenial either to the traditionalist Christian view or to the fashionable secularist view. Basically, I take my start from the historicity of Christ. While I find it very difficult to put any meaning into the word God in a general way, I do not find it difficult to recognize a historical demand upon me in the historicity of Christ. In brief, I consider that in Christ we have the message of true secularity. Christ was the truly secular man. He was free from the old world, bound absolutely to his Father, and thus free for the authentic historicity of this world. In his life there does not appear the theological abstraction of a double world, the world of nature and the world of supernature, or the appreciation of a sacred and a profane order of life. But he appears as free from the old world, free of gods. The world is one, and it is the Father's, and because it is the Father's it is the son's. But the son is not merely the man for others. But he is the exponent of the way, that is, he is the very way in which co-humanity may be lived as something more than co-humanity.

This 'something more' is not something suprahistorical. Briefly, I should call it a new reality of transcendence and a new reality of spirit within history. It is a new reality of transcendence, in that we are here faced with the otherness of God not as a theory of the world, but as a historical encounter. 'Inasmuch as you have done it unto the least of these my brethren, you have done it unto me' (Matt. 17). But this reality of otherness can also be described as a new reality of spirit. Man's humanity is therefore not constituted simply by his being active for other men, in co-

151

humanity, but also by his recognizing in his activity a realm which does not belong either to himself alone or to his fellow-men with him. This is the realm of the spirit, the realm which lies between men, and in this realm all man's possibilities are concentrated.

This is not the same as a spiritualizing of man's history, but it is a hope for man which both includes and surpasses (transcends) the individual. It includes him in his absolute irreplace-ability—and because of this we are bound to do all we can for the betterment of the individual's existence—and it surpasses the individual in that it does not see the end merely in the immanent possibilities of history. But it recognizes the end of man in the affirmation of a reality which is both entirely human and also more than the sum of all humanity: this is the reality of spirit, and it is this reality which we name with the word 'God'.

How this view may be related to the traditional theological view of God as the wholly other who has made an irruption into human history, I cannot enter into here. The traditional views are deeply infected by mythological thought-forms, and need interpretation all along the line. What I wish to maintain is that it is in Christ, and in a consequent christological view of history, that we may find our understanding of man's destiny. A merely theistic world-view is not enough. It is even questionable whether a theistic world-view is essential for a Christ-centred view of history. But it is not enough to put Christ so much into the centre of the picture that God becomes an abstraction.[1] On the other hand, the old transcendentalist metaphysic is settled and finished. It is basically an objectifying of God and no more than an extension of our own world, which is given in the traditional world-view.

Perhaps all that we can hope for today is the preparation and

[1] As Körner does, cf. *Zeitschrift für Theologie und Kirche* December 1966.

expectation of a new world picture, perhaps even a philosophy, which might incorporate more satisfactorily the basic Christian insights. Whether this happens or not, one thing I am sure of, and that is that Christian faith need not be diffident. It is based upon a message which is both historical and eschatological: the substance of Christian faith is its confidence in the paradoxical unity of historical facts and eschatological reality. This message does not lead away from the world, but right into it. It speaks to man, and about man. It offers him a hope which at the same time preserves all his historical possibilities, and yet overcomes the ultimate boundaries of human existence. It overcomes them in the sense that it recognizes the givenness of everything. The theological word for this is grace. 'I saw the goodness of the Lord in the land of the living.'[1]

What I have said provides no more than pointers to the way we must think of faith and of God and of the world. In conclusion, I think it is important to recognize that Christianity is not a philosophical system. It is in truth an immense operation of reduction upon all thinking, upon all religion, upon all the multitude of possibilities which appear to man in his undecided state. It is a particular faith which is a particular response to a particular address. The philosophical consequences of this faith operate at different times in different ways. But the reality of the address, and the real possibility of the response, do not vary. It is in this sense that we can reiterate the words of the writer to the Hebrews: Jesus Christ the same yesterday and today and for ever.

Whether this means that a new Christian philosophy must speak not of God but only of Christ, is a question which modern theology must tackle. For my part I consider that a *theologia negativa* has an important part to play. We speak of historicity and man and his responsibility—and rightly so. We do this in

[1]Psalm 27.13.

153

terms of the empirical reality of Christ and of faith through him. But we must also speak of mystery and reserve. Mystery even when we face our fellow-men, silence even when we attempt to describe those we know and love best. How much more so when we try to speak of God? He is the hinterland behind every truly human interrelation. But to describe him means either that we say nothing or we say that he is nothing. But this *nihil* is not the orphaned horror of Jean Paul's vision in *Siebenkäs*, nor the flagrant defiance of Nietzsche's challenge. But it is the *nihil* of the *Ungrund* which is simply the intensification, by analogy, of the mystery of all human existence and all human interrelation.

Co-humanity carries with it the unavoidable historical reality of inter-humanity, and inter-humanity points unavoidably to the reality of God, as with us, for us, in us, and yet not of us. We cannot objectify God and we cannot speak directly of him. Too much theology is too familiar with God, and too anxious to enclose him in a doctrine or a system. All such attempts either lead us simply back to ourselves, by a detour over the objects which we propose to describe him by, or they lead us into mere immanentism. In either way we do not get beyond objects in this world. It is only in the strength of faith which includes an acknowledgement of transcendence as the heart of the event of co-humanity, that we may actually approach God: the living God, the God of Abraham and Isaac and Jacob: but we may approach him because he has made himself approachable, as far as that is possible at all, through our fellow-men.

The reality of God for us is thus a historical reality, and nothing besides. But this does not mean a God who becomes, nor on the other hand does it mean a mere abstraction from the historical Christ. But the history of man appears now as the history of his dialogue with God. Sometimes this takes very strange forms, so that God is entirely hidden behind the structures of history. Then we may speak of an eclipse of God, and all we can do is wait patiently. The form of hope may thus take the expression of agnosticism or atheism. But sometimes, again, the moment burns, and God is present as a fearful conviction, as a Face in the midst of our encounters with our fellow-men. This is the moment for which faith hopes. But in its hope faith does not let go of its endless criticism of all science and all controlled planning of the future. For in the last analysis there is no planning or control possible, beyond the faith that hopes for the encounter with God as the power of all history. This means that at bottom faith is responsible for history, but God is responsible for faith: everything for man lies therefore in the unpredictable future of God.

INDEX OF NAMES